JUNK SHOP
WINDOW

JUNK SHOP WINDOW

ESSAYS ON
MYTH, LIFE, AND LITERATURE

James J. Patterson

Alan Squire Publishing
Bethesda, Maryland

Alan Squire Publishing

Junk Shop Window is published by Alan Squire Publishing, Bethesda, MD, an imprint of the Santa Fe Writers Project.

Printed in the United States of America.
ISBN (print): 978-1-942892-34-2
ISBN (epub): 978-1-942892-35-9

Library of Congress Control Number: 2022951102

Jacket design and cover art by Randy Stanard.
Author photo by Rose Solari.
Copy editing and interior design by Nita Congress.
Printing consultant: Steven Waxman.

Printed by Carter Printing Company.

First Edition
Ordo Vagorum

ALSO BY JAMES J. PATTERSON:

Bermuda Shorts (essays)

Roughnecks (a novel)

For Rose

TABLE OF CONTENTS

Introduction, by Nathan Leslie 1

PART I: THE MEMORY OF TOMORROW

Hermes and the Bathtub 7

The Memory of Tomorrow 13

A St. Patrick's Day Schmazzle 21

The I Behind the I 31

Do Conservatives Dream of an Electric Jesus? 39

Digby at the Swan 49

The Band That Time Forgot 63

Throwing in the Tao 67

PART II: THE WORLD OF YESTERDAY

Who's a Good Boy? 79

Hermes at the Spouter Inn 87

While Writing *Roughnecks* and Reading
Moby Dick 103

The World of Yesterday 113

Stirring the Pot on Henry Miller. 133

Hermes at the Kakistocracy Hotel 151

I'm the Guy Who (Almost) Killed the Guy Who
(Almost) Killed Albert Einstein. 161

Acknowledgments

Works Cited

INTRODUCTION

by Nathan Leslie

W hat exactly *is* an essay? Upon each reading of a collection of essays, I end up with the same question. This has to do with the nature of the form—part excavation, part journal entry, part journalism, part op-ed. The literary essay, at its best, is a smattering of all of these. Even within a single occurrence, an essay may vacillate between all possible manifestations. In fact, the best essays do—they capture the world by part and parcel, both itself and the individual's place in it.

James J. Patterson's *Junk Shop Window* does just this—and then some.

The all-inclusiveness of Patterson's aesthetic within this collection is something to behold, as it was in his previous *Bermuda Shorts* of 2010. Not only does he capture his own life (for instance, his wife Rose appears as a frequent "character" in these works, often offering insights or bon mots from just offstage), but he also diligently renders what he is reading and thinking about, and connects what he is reading and thinking about, to the world at large. Within these pages William Wordsworth and Henry Miller—both of whom one might think, at first, are passé in 2023—are fervently, *urgently* relevant again. Here Herman Melville and Pascal Mercier and Fernando Pessoa and Arthur Conan Doyle still live among us. Books live here; authors live here; words matter. And Patterson is here to tell us how and why—yet sans rant, sans pedantry, sans showy allusiveness.

Within this collection, mythology, especially the figure of Hermes, appears. Though in the twenty-first century many may neglect to ponder ancient Greek and Roman mythology, Patterson brings this figure to contemporary relevance. Hermes is the messenger to the gods, just as Patterson is the messenger to our ears and eyes. He beckons: Follow these words and you too shall make discoveries and linkages.

This is a difficult balance to strike: the past and the present commingling; memory and experiences living on the page concurrently. In this collection, encounters with strangers are as important as the books in Patterson's library. Patterson's stunning and poetic utilization of onomatopoeia within these essays juxtaposes with the more internal search for self (soul?). Take the essay "Do Conservatives Dream of an Electric Jesus?" (what titles!). Within this piece, Patterson investigates our current fascination with apocalyptic narratives, especially cinematic ones. He contextualizes *Blade Runner*'s popularity and impact in the milieu of the rise of Reaganism and Evangelicalism. "A New Feudalism is dawning," Patterson writes. "And it is right at our door." Indeed. What is striking about such an account is not just the analysis, but the artful manner in which Patterson brings the argument home to his own personal lived experience. It is as if Patterson read my mind here: I too am sick of apocalyptic tropes. Here we are in the world as it is, the author suggests—how will we navigate this terrain?

Or take the essay "The I Behind the I," which skillfully provides a bridge between poets of yesteryear and visiting chums. It is theory meets praxis. It is the bookshelf as tool. Books and authors and words don't just matter in and of themselves, but also as a way of understanding the landscape around us. The author is at his best when connecting past to present in this way. In this regard Patterson takes a page out of Ralph Waldo Emerson, with perhaps a dash of Michel de Montaigne, the sixteenth-century philosopher regarded by many as the father of the personal essay.

The reader will notice that humor and music both appear as frequent motifs within these pieces. Patterson was one-half of the D.C.-based folk band The Pheromones, who spent fifteen years touring the country and produced four popular CDs. Within this book, you will find a piece in which he plays a fly on the musical wall to this experience. Another essay originated as the liner notes for a double album, *Then and Now*, by the North Star Band. Given the musicality of the language here, one is unsurprised at the musical dimension of the author's life and interests.

As for humor—it is the dark matter of this book, everywhere and all at once! This may be the greatest through line of all throughout this collection. The humor has to do with the voice of these essays, the playful use of hyperbole and metaphor, the singular descriptions, the nicknames, and Patterson's skewering of sacred cows. Patterson may be a scholar of Wordsworth, but he thankfully fails to take himself too seriously, while always taking *words* themselves seriously.

There is no pat answer to the question I proposed in paragraph one. The personal essay is perhaps a catch-all, a mishmash without set expectations (and if such expectations existed, it would make the form far less dynamic anyway). At times, literary essays may make us think of Substack, of blogs, of online articles that make the stuff of the Internet churn. Yet read an entire collection of such artfully crafted insights—through the accumulated effect, there is much more here than a haphazard assemblage. *Junk Shop Window* is an album of ideas. Here are words to let reverberate in your ears. Read, listen, and you shall learn.

PART I

THE MEMORY OF TOMORROW

HERMES AND THE BATHTUB

t was four in the morning on a weekday.

When I woke up I was behind the wheel in a van full of newspapers going eighty miles an hour down a quiet small-town neighborhood street. It was a seven-day-a-week job and it had been several months, maybe a year, since my last day off.

The guy I had brought to keep me awake was fast asleep in the passenger seat. We didn't wear seat belts because we normally spent all night stopping and starting, jumping in and out of the vehicle dropping bundles. We were in a V8-powered box made of double-plated U.S. steel and we were moving really fast.

Two telephone poles later—one down on the street, the other on top of the van, both throwing live wires this way and that, and a parked station wagon bent in half—I was pulled from the burning vehicle by that same helper, now fully awake, having been spared by the wall of ten-pound bundles of newsprint that fell down on him when we hit the first pole. He ripped my head back from where it was lodged in the steering wheel, gripping my torso under my dislocated shoulders, and pulled me through a shattered window. As a matter of fact, I remember distinctly, as that second pole rushed up to meet us and now directly in front of me and knowing I was about to die, thinking, simply and calmly, "What a shame."

Six weeks or more later I was back on my feet, if a little tenuous on my pins, with a cane to support my mangled left leg, when something quite alarming began occurring in my lower regions. The urologist said that part of my body had gone into post-traumatic shock, and a condition called epididymitis set in (you'll have to look it up, as I'm not going to describe it here, suffice to say that the family jewels had swelled to the size of a very healthy pomegranate). The doctor told me that there were no drugs that could get to that part of the body to alleviate my discomfort or get me back to normal, but there was a good chance that rendering that part of my body warm and weightless for several hours a day might have a calming and healing effect. The doctor prescribed five one-hour-long baths each day, as hot as I could stand them, and advised me to make whatever might cause stress in my life to go away. I remember laughing to myself, thinking that would mean tell everybody I know to get lost!

So, on my way home from the doctor to begin another six-week ordeal of recuperation, and realizing that I was not only going to be laid up once more but that I was also to be hot water–logged as well, I pulled into my favorite bookstore at the time, Brentano's, and decided to stock up for the deluge.

And so, I found myself staring at a wall of science fiction the like of which I haven't seen before or since.

Brentano's, if you don't know, was a marvelous small chain of large bookstores—large meaning about five thousand square feet, more or less. Their selection of classic fiction and portables seemed endless, and their sci-fi section took up an entire wall. To someone not truly familiar with the genre, that was daunting. But I was in the mood for the fantastic, not the stark and very real. I had just had a big dose of that, and that was plenty for me.

I had loved sci-fi movies when I was a kid, loved the comic books and paperback magazines too. I had read Jules Verne and H.G. Wells when I was a young reader, but once I fell in love with Dickens, then Steinbeck, then Hesse, then the romantic poets, my reading was as far from the genre as it could be. As I stood there gazing at this wall of colorful, sensational, gaudy-looking book covers, big fat trilogies, anthologies of epic off-world adventures, I decided now would be a perfect time to acquaint myself with a few titles. But I was at a real loss. I wanted in, but I would need a guide.

I've always felt a kinship with the notion that the gods often appear to us, momentarily, in the guise of amicable strangers.

You have experienced this: suddenly someone steps out of a crowd, out of nowhere, and gives you an unsolicited piece of information, or advice, or an idea, then he or she slips away. It's over so fast you just pause momentarily. If you remember the event at all, you may even think you dreamed it.

I have also wondered what in the world one might call such a creature. A creature who could take possession of a living breathing human being for the sole purpose of telling someone else something they need to know. I don't think there's a patron saint of mysterious hint givers. Or a secret league of cryptic messengers. Well, come to think of it, maybe there is one. Nevertheless, the god I can most closely associate with this phenomenon is the trickster messenger god Hermes.

Maybe I can better explain by describing this kind of happening in reverse. When *you* are suddenly overcome with an overpowering urge to tell someone you don't know something they hadn't thought of. Possessed of an idea, in an elevator say, or the subway, or moving along with a slow-moving crowd. You see just the right person; they pause. A remark, an observation, a pithy piece of advice is ready to leap off your tongue; you call it out. And suddenly it's you who are the messenger. You have become Hermes, if only for an instant. Know it or not, you've done that too.

By no means am I a scholar of mythology. I will, however, pounce on new translations of Homer (Fagles is still my fav, but Emily Wilson has recently turned my head). I have always found First Nation and Native American nature deities fascinating, as well as Vedic seers and Haitian spirit-guardians of the crossroads. So, I'm open to the concept that we sometimes communicate on levels even we ourselves don't fully understand.

So, there I was, standing before that inscrutable wall of sci-fi feeling lost and bewildered but knowing that the secret to my next six weeks was right in front of me would that I had eyeballs with which to see it.

Enter Hermes.

Feeling a presence near me I turned, and there he was. A Vietnam vet, clearly; they were everywhere in those days. He was about my age, perhaps three or four years older, wearing his worn and tattered army fatigues, long unkempt hair, boots. He held a cane to reinforce a damaged left leg, same as me. He wasn't looking at the wall of books; he had already made his purchase. He was looking at me, and clearly aware of my bewilderment.

I looked at the wall, then back at him, then at the book he held in his hand, a very fat paperback, and I said, "You look like someone who might know his way down this Great Wall of Titles."

"Oh, I've read almost all of them, all the good ones that is," he smiled. When I explained that I was new and didn't want to just grab stuff that looked interesting, he entirely agreed. Said I would invariably pick something terrible, take it home and hate it, then never read another. "Would you like me to recommend a few?"

I remember that what struck me was the sudden formal tone to his question, and I realized he was trying to ascertain whether or not I was serious or just making conversation. When I assured him I was indeed serious and shared a brief account of my situation, he seemed charmed and for the better part of an hour he calmly gave me his breakdown of what clearly to him was more than a reader's delight. It was a devotion.

"It begins and ends here," he said reverently, handing me a recently published single-volume oversized paperback of the three books comprising Isaac Asimov's *Foundation Trilogy*. A few years later I would recognize Asimov's universe as the backdrop to a new film called *Star Wars*, and just about every other space adventure I've enjoyed since then.

Another book he plucked from the shelf was *Dune*, by Frank Herbert. "If you're going to be in the tub that much, you might enjoy reading about a world where there's no water, a desert world with sandworms as big as dinosaurs, and everybody's hooked on a spice that turns the whites of their eyes blue."

Yes, I just might be interested in a world like that. (Herbert had yet to bastardize his classic with several lesser sequels. Hey, we all gotta eat.)

Another book he chose was by Jack London, of all people. *The Star Rover* is about a man in a straightjacket in the dungeon of a prison having out-of-body experiences, where he visits his past lives, which he is living simultaneously. "It might help you get outta that tub, without actually getting out of that tub," he smiled.

That young vet turned me on to *Stranger in a Strange Land*, by Robert Heinlein, and the word *grok*, basically a synonym for *to understand*, as well as books by Harlan Ellison, Andre Alice Norton, Piers Anthony, and many others I still pick up and read today.

As I gathered up this armful of loot and made my way to the checkout counter, I looked around the store, but my mentor was gone.

It had started to rain, not heavily, and I tucked my huge bundle of books under my arm inside my buckskin jacket and, cane in hand, stepped outside.

A few paces down the street he was suddenly at my side once more. Before I could say anything, he reached into a satchel he carried over his shoulder and pulled out the same book he had been holding when we met. It was obviously the book he had come to the store to buy that afternoon. A giant book of short stories edited, I think, by Robert Heinlein. "Most everybody who's anybody is in this book," he said, and handed it to me. When I looked at him, slightly stunned, he said simply, "To thank you for asking," and he turned, hobbled off down the street, and we went our separate ways in the rain. I never knew his name. But he turned those hundreds of hours I spent in that scalding hot tub into a literary adventure that changed my life, and that I still draw upon to this day. Once again, thank you my friend. Whatever became of you, I hope you were appreciated.

FYI, the baths worked.

The Memory of Tomorrow

t is ten till two a.m. on a Thursday morning in late January. A winter storm has temporarily cut off the power. Many candles burn. The candlelight loves the heavy red velvet curtains, the cranberry wallpaper with images—all the color of copper turned teal green—of nymphs and flower urns. A stick of amber incense adds a subtle sweetness to the atmosphere, an atmosphere that wants poetry and good red wine.

Rose sleeps upstairs. The house is quiet, the neighborhood is quiet, in the way only a slow heavy snowfall can hush the world. It's the memory of quiet that makes me look up from my book to take in the candlelight. The quiet invokes a familiar feeling. It's a feeling I realize I've had many times before, but once it passes, I forget about it until it returns. And as I return to my reading, reveling in the delicious cadences of long, well-written poems, the ingenuity of revealed wisdoms, the unexpected turns of thought that can surprise even after many readings over many years, I am suddenly aware of a background ambiance. Pausing to listen, I recognize it, a comforting sound, familiar all the way to my bones. I smile and return to my reading when I suddenly have the kind of wait-a-minute revelation I will often have when I detect that something is very out of order. Because the sound that has comforted me late at night at times like this, throughout my life, is not possible. It is the clippity-clop sound of a horse, trotting on cobblestones in the snow, pulling a small carriage, in the night.

The book I'm reading falls to the floor.

Almost worried, partly amused, I stand, and walk to the window. I can see snow falling slow and steady between the houses. I go to the front door, pull it open, and step out onto the sheltered front step. The cold is thrilling. Breathing it in has a purifying effect on my lungs. Was I half expecting to see gas lamps out on the street and a carriage coming up the hill in the snow? Maybe I was. But the power is out, and all is hush and dark. The snow falling has the soft sound of air moving gently. It tastes like electricity.

Sometimes a snowfall like this one actually warms the air somewhat, friction I suppose. But it is too cold to stand here all night, although I want to. The veil between worlds has become very thin—how do I know that? Because each of my senses is being called to it, the senses I know and think I can direct, and the ones I'm not aware of. They are searching for a thread after taking a hint. In this state I doubt anything could surprise me. If an ancestor I've not heard of, maybe one who looks a little like me, male or female, or even some hound or other animal familiar, should step out of the falling snow and hand me something I need, or impart a piece of advice, warning, or merely a comfort, I would accept it. If that creature stepped out of the snow and demanded a gift, I would give it. I turn my head slowly side to side, encouraging those senses to reach out and explore. I am tempted to make a slow sideways movement, like a tai chi gesture, a secret step, and if I do it properly an open-sesame will occur. I will see the Pythagorean angles in time all around, and, if I want to, I could slip between them, becoming myself an adumbration. And I would be standing in another time. Another now. As another me.

Pleasant voices echo quietly from a short distance away in the falling snow, their words not quite discernible to me. It's as if, in this half-space, this odd moment, so random and rare, I'm home. I know these people.

They know me. There is love here. But I'm on the front porch of my house late of a wintery night, it's 2019, I'm older, the love of my life is upstairs quietly sleeping, and I'm happy. Happier than I've ever been. And I can hear the snow-muffled clippity-clop of the horse and carriage as though it were coming from behind and beyond those dark, quiet houses across the street, the sound slowly fading into the snow. I want to walk out into the night and follow this. I don't dare. The chill finally penetrates my heavy sweater and jeans.

Back inside, I remember lying in my bed as a child, on a night like this, hearing that noise while watching the snow-flakes pass through the light from the street lamp out my bedroom window. Then, I'm middle-aged, at a pensione in Verona; I get up in the middle of the night and run to the window and see nothing in the street but parked cars. Then in my late twenties in a spooky old house in central Ontario, Canada, the moonlight bright through the window turning everything blue, there it is again. In many different places and settings have I had this subconscious experience, now brought vividly forward in my mind. Each time taking for granted that such a sound, even the impossibility of it, was normal. Like it was as natural as any other sound that might occur in the middle of the night, in winter, when you're alone with your mind.

Lately, in books and magazines, I have noticed philosophers and physicists revisiting the idea that all time happens simultaneously. That there is no yesterday or tomorrow, there is only the now. That the other lives you may have led, you are actually leading now, at the same time. That the places you go in your dreams are the places your other selves inhabit, and the people you meet in those dreams reside there, too. But in the here and now, those people pass in your dreams as random imaginings, or bits of memory in collage. When first I was exposed to that notion, I instantly felt that it was true. It explains déjà vu, precognitive dreams, premonitions, and perhaps a lot more.

People depended upon horses for thousands of years. The new houses across my street are in a development called The Mews. Was there a public stable there once upon a time? My parents were old enough to remember being young when people still used horses to get around. So, it really wasn't that long ago.

In my early twenties, a girlfriend gave me a set of Sherlock Holmes mysteries. I devoured them. But what I found so enchanting wasn't necessarily the charming characters of Holmes and Watson, though charming they be, nor was it the clever and complicated plots and the unpredictable solutions they inspired, nor was it the clean, clear prose Conan Doyle used to harness his fictional structures. No, it was the transport into that strange world of late nineteenth-century London I found so mesmerizing. Candlelight, a slow-smoldering fireplace, dense pipe tobacco, musty crowded bookshelves that sit heavy in the room. Dressing every day in tweeds, cotton, starched shirts, heavy sweaters, hats that fit well, shielded the eyes, and kept one's head warm and dry. The smells of horsehide and dung, burning coal, claret, good port or strong whiskey, overtaking the senses. Where everything is made from iron, steel, tin, heavy leather, and good hardwood. Is my suddenly hearing a horse-drawn carriage an atavistic feeling? What else could it be? Is a quiet late-night snowfall an ambient trigger to memories stored in my DNA?

After falling in love with the Arthur Conan Doyle stories, I quit my job, and at the suggestion of a radio disc jockey who lived across the hall, I decided to recreate some of those Holmes stories as audio dramas for the radio. I thought I was going to be the next Orson Welles.

At about two or three in the morning, the studio director where I was recording my adaptations called to say, "Jimmy, get over here!" When I arrived, he had set up his microphones on an upstairs balcony. We had been trying to get an open-air ambiance for those outdoor scenes we were creating, and getting that without cars or airplanes or any modern indicators was almost impossible. But this night was quiet, with no traffic. It was so still, in fact, that we sat in the studio like a great pair of fools, listening to nothing in the middle of the night, and the needles on the recording studio's machines weren't moving at all. So, I went out onto the balcony and howled like an old dog, and lo and behold, dogs from all the neighborhoods around began barking back, creating just enough echo to register on the machines.

I'm thinking this and using that memory to analyze the sounds I think I'm hearing now from behind the snowfall outside. No, I conclude, there is no rational explanation for what I'm hearing. I'm hearing hoofbeats, damn it.

Clip-clop clip-clop clip-clop.

I pour some wine and return to my book of poems. But this strange revelation regarding what I have been hearing, or not hearing, has put me in a mood of nervous disquiet, and never until this moment did I find it odd in any way, which is, of course, odd.

I put down the book again. Maybe it's these damn poems that do this to me, I laugh to myself, as I reach for my journal.

Not long ago I would have sat down and written someone a letter. I used to write dozens of letters as a way to warm up to a writing session. I would write a letter to a friend, then write basically that same letter to a second friend, and then perhaps a third to a third, growing my ideas and the nature of my inquiries with customized alterations depending on each individual recipient's circumstances, while remaining conscientious about how those circumstances did or did not bump up against my own. Within a few weeks, postcards, letters containing long, off-topic, free associations, even books on related subjects, would start arriving in the mail. These communications benefited by being gradual rather than immediate. Mind you, reciprocity from my pen pals was always weak in volume if not in substance. What's worse is that since the publication of my first book of essays, those old chums have taken it upon themselves to do me the favor of returning to me my many correspondences from over the years (I was astonished to learn they had kept them).

There's a kind of morbid finality to opening a packet containing your own letters, some written as far back as forty years ago. It occurs to me that the letter I would have written tonight, normally addressed to an intimate yet innocent bystander, is the page beneath my pen right now. Is it for my son? Maybe. To a grandchild living or unborn? Perhaps a great-grandchild may take an interest in these pages. But I doubt it. Perhaps that's as it should be, these late-night meanderings are somehow more accessible when approached with indifference. As if they will be placed and ultimately found in some sort of Tomorrow Box, left for an unknown apprentice to help decipher and decode.

A friend asked me once if his turning fifty was too late for him to begin a journal. "Of course not, you may live another thirty years, so explore your thoughts and experiences." I gave him a few pointers. "Above all, don't bitch. Include sights, sounds, and the other senses. Write down what people say. And remember, someday, someone might read it. They will find it in the Tomorrow Box you build each day. Keep whomever that might be in mind. Be nice to them. They might be the last person on Earth to ever fall in love with you."

Initially, in my writing, I intended to merely explore my own mind, because without this process, most ideas and inquiries will flicker by and then extinguish themselves, unexamined.

Like hearing the clippity-clop of horses trotting in the snow.

I get up one more time and step toward the front door. Perhaps this time I will take that side-eye turn, but the power comes back on with a sudden flash of lights. Music resumes playing from the living room, the furnace in the basement thunders back to life, a television somewhere starts hollering. I turn most everything off, returning the house to quietude and candlelight. I finish my wine and the poem I was reading and go upstairs. Rose is still purring like a kitten. I crawl into bed beside her. And as I yawn and stretch and settle in, I see out the bedroom window snowflakes gently falling through the beam from the street lamp outside, and as all returns to darkness and quiet the comforting clip-clop, clip-clop, clip-clop, of a lone horse in the muffled distance returns, gently pulling a carriage through the snow, creating a backbeat that carries me all the way into tomorrow.

A St. Patrick's Day Schmazzle

At the time this tale I'm about to tell unfolds, my mother, Dorothy Rose, was still alive and wintering in Florida. Usually, by mid-March she would be hankering to return to her native Canada for the spring and summer months, and would monitor weekly, then daily, weather reports from her up-north pals on the rate at which the snow was melting. Once her calculations were set, her activities would center around the gradual closing of one abode and the opening of the other. On this occasion, she phoned me up in Washington, D.C., and said that if I wanted a quiet place to write for a few weeks, I could come down, help her get packed up to head north, and then I could have her house all to myself for a spell. Of course, it would be summer in Florida, meaning hot, hot, hot, but, hey, she was on the Gulf and had a small kidney-shaped pool, in a neighborhood festooned with palm trees.

Shade. Ocean. And a pool.

I'll get by, somehow.

Yes, it all looked good on paper, and Washington, D.C., can be a stifling hell-hole in the summer if you're in your late twenties and can't afford air conditioning. First, a little bit about Mom. You know breeds of herding dogs who are small in

21

stature but with big hearts, cheerful, attentive, alert, self-motivated, who, without anyone realizing it, will circle around until they have you all in a group, or have moved you from one place to another? Well, that was Mom; adorable, enthusiastic, and indefatigable, with big brown eyes that were hard to say no to.

I invited my old grade-school pal, Willy, on my excursion to the Sunshine State. Willy liked doing chores. I knew he'd roll up his sleeves as soon as he touched down and I, for one, would be happy to let him. When Mom headed north, he'd head west to a summer farming gig. Peace and quiet were right around the corner.

I wouldn't even have been friends with Willy if, in the fourth grade, Mom hadn't seen us walking home from school together.

I was one of the smallest kids in school and Willy was one of the biggest. I generally kept to myself because when you're small, everyone is a bully. As a result, I didn't make friends. The only reason Willy and I were walking down the street together at all was that I had caught up with him on the sidewalk in front of school to lace him out about his comportment in class. He had come over from a nearby public school to our Catholic one and had some undisciplined habits that needed correcting. First and foremost was his habit of calling out the answers in class. I was so painfully shy, it was all I could do to raise my hand when the teacher asked a question.

"And if you're just going to blurt out the answer every damn time, it leaves the rest of us in the lurch. So cut it out!"

Just then Mom pulled up in her station wagon. Overjoyed at seeing me conversing with another student, she threw open the passenger-side car door and told us both to get in, she'd give him a ride home. He hopped in front, I got in back. There was no getting her attention. She wouldn't read my look. A look that said "What are you doing! I hate this guy!"

It was a Friday, and the next thing I knew she was introducing herself to his mom and inviting the brute home with us for the weekend!

Twenty years, and a thousand and one adventures later, she greeted us at her house in Florida with great plates of food and a bottle of Canadian rye whiskey. She killed the bottle of whiskey with us late into the night as we got caught up, then sent us to our rooms. She had us up six hours later to a great breakfast and a list of chores.

And she had arranged a treat. My buddy's name was William Zachary Harper and his Irish bona fides were solid, right down to his dark Irish rugby player looks, several broken noses included. But, unlike every Irish American I've ever known, Willy was clueless on the subject of Irish American cultural characteristics. He would waltz into an Irish pub and order up a Heineken; he couldn't tell a Guinness from a bottle of ink. Still, Mom's good news was she had three tickets for us to see the Irish Rovers concert at the new Van Wezel arena that very evening. Happy Saint Patrick's Day, boys!

Also, each year as she prepared to go north, she would purchase spring training baseball tickets for however many of her Canadian friends were in town. On this occasion, there happened to be twenty-seven snowbirds in town eager to attend, and the Canadian Major League Baseball team, the Toronto Blue Jays, were in town to face the Chicago White Sox. So, concert that night, baseball game the following afternoon.

Life was good.

So, chores done, an early dinner in our bellies, we made ready for the Irish Rovers.

Up until recently, Willy and I had shared a group house back in Washington, and the Rovers were a regular on our turntable.

I'm a rambler, I'm a gambler, I'm a long way from home
And if you don't like me, then leave me alone,
I'll eat when I'm hungry, I'll drink when I'm dry
And if moonshine don't kill me, I'll live 'til I die.

We were singing all afternoon.

When we made ready to leave for the concert, Mom produced a bag of Irish flare.

On Willy she pinned a giant button the size of a dinner plate that read KISS ME I'M IRISH!

On my head she placed a giant straw hat with a three-foot-long green ostrich feather that bobbed and waggled insanely about, and a dozen buttons with varying pro-Irish messages.

For herself she donned a big green sash, like from a beauty pageant, that reached from left shoulder to right hip and read ERIN GO BRAGH!

In its day, the Van Wezel Performing Arts Hall was the Gulf Coast's answer to Sydney's Opera house, in miniature. A purple sea shell, just ostentatious enough to be cool, sort of, especially in Florida, where brightly colored polyester was all in vogue.

As we entered the concert hall, which appeared to be sold out, I was baffled to see that most of the patrons were way overdressed. Evening gowns, jewelry, sport coats and leather shoes. Wealthy Republicans liked the Irish Rovers?

When you're young and out with your parents, you generally assume that a certain amount of embarrassment with a pinch of humiliation just naturally comes with the endeavor. So yeah, I was the guy whose mom put him in a big dumb hat and a long green feather, and still, I was blind to the clues of impending disaster that were all around me.

Mom led the way, platinum blond, a solid, curvy five-two, one hundred and thirty pounds, burrowing through the lobby crowd. When we got to the theater entrance, she couldn't find the tickets. This was totally predictable, and I amused myself concocting an escape plan should the tickets not be found. We would adjourn to a nearby restaurant, one that catered to the theater crowd, have some libations, then hear what actual, ticket-holding concertgoers had to say as they came rolling in when the show was over. Meanwhile, she, then Willy and she, then Willy and she and the elderly volunteer taking tickets all had a turn searching through her purse, until the tickets were found.

Inside the hall, the elderly usher couldn't read the tickets and said the seats must be upstairs. The usher upstairs couldn't read them either and suggested the seats must be up at the top balcony. At the top, the usher couldn't read them either and, eyeing Willy and I, beaming back at him in all our green bling, figured the tickets were up in the last row where seats are discounted for college students.

We made the climb. We grabbed three empty seats. The house lights came down. A bright spotlight appeared at the curtain, stage right. And out onto the stage strolled Tony Bennett.

Tony Bennett.

Mom?

As I was trying to get my head around the fact that Tony Bennett was somehow opening for the Irish Rovers, an usher with young healthy eyes approached us with three agitated concertgoers behind him, and demanded to see our tickets.

"These are baseball tickets, ma'am."

Baseball tickets?

Just then, a very familiar voice sang out, "I left my heart in San Francisco..." to the roar of the crowd.

"Oh, my God!" Dorothy exclaimed as we were being escorted out, inching our way past seated patrons, with our bling blinging, and my giant feather waggling insanely.

"High on a hill, it calls to me..."

Willy and I suddenly got the giggles. Dorothy was holding it together like a good materfamilias, but we couldn't look at her.

We descended several levels, returning to the lobby, my giant feather bobbing and weaving, Willy giggling like a delinquent, and Mom in a hurry. I was having none of it, making for the exit with my usual subsonic determination.

"Stop right there, Jimmy Patterson, we're not going anywhere. We've got to find those ticket stubs!"

"Ticket stubs? Who cares about ticket stubs?" I was making a beeline out of there and thanking God I was the keeper of the car keys.

Willy caught up with me in the parking lot as I was nearing the car.

"We've gotta get back in there and find those stubs or three people won't be going to the game tomorrow!"

At this point I could've cared less if anyone in the world ever went to another baseball game again. But Willy dragged me back to the theater where Mom, and two or three volunteer ushers, had upended all the ticket boxes and were on their hands and knees on the lobby floor searching through enormous piles of little bits of paper ticket stubs for the other half of Mom's baseball tickets.

I bought myself a wine from the concession volunteers and hung with a couple of other aged ushers discussing the relative merits of more frequent eye examinations, and the dubious prospects of their Medicare plans taking care of it, as we watched the activities on the floor where Mom and her newly recruited gray brigade were on all fours, searching for the tickets.

Meanwhile the theater manager arrived on the scene, where Mom began lacing him out royally.

"What do you mean the Rovers are here next week, today is St. Patrick's Day!"

"Yes, ma'am, but you see, the Rovers are on a tour, they don't only just play on St. Patrick's Day."

"Nonsense!"

They found one ticket stub.

Dorothy's ass was chapped.

"Who in hell, what kind of idiot, hires the Irish Rovers for the week *AFTER* St. Patty's Day!?! And where are my other two damned tickets!?"

I handed her my wine.

"Dorothy, Dorothy, Dorothy" (I began calling my parents by their first names on my sixteenth birthday; they rebelled at first, but I have always maintained that it had a levelling, humanizing effect on them, and saved my life), "Dorothy, listen please. Willy and I can get our own tickets, and you take the one found ticket. Boom, problem solved. Now let's leave these nice folks before the intermission comes, please?" Mom reluctantly agreed to abandon the search. But Dorothy Rose had a few parting words for the manager as he was escorting us through the door.

"Well, we've been thrown out of better places than this!" she barked as she got in the car.

"Come to think of it, Mrs. P., I don't think I *have* been thrown out of a better place than this," Willy scratched his head.

"I can't remember ever being thrown out of anywhere," I shook my head, thinking back. "No, I stand corrected, there were several classrooms."

We adjourned to the aforementioned restaurant. And by the time we got there the three of us were laughing so hard we could hardly contain ourselves. As our drinks arrived, Dorothy suddenly stopped laughing, looked suspiciously at me and said, "Wait a minute Jimmy, you were going to leave us there?"

"I should have. But don't worry, I would have called a cab to bring you here."

"How thoughtful."

"Either that or I was just going to pull around front, put the flashers on, then run inside like a madman and drag you both out by the hair."

"You shut up, Jimmy Patterson."

Then it was back to the house, and another bottle of Canadian rye bit the dust.

Next day, Willy and I arrived at the ballpark in the middle of the first inning. A scalper in the parking lot sold us bleacher seats along the first base line, two for the price of one. Across the diamond, along the third base line, sat the twenty-seven Canadians sitting in a square formation chattering, laughing, and drinking beer, stuffing their faces and having a ball. They were easy to spot by the guy in the straw hat with a big tall green feather waggling crazily in the breeze. That was Mr. Kay, a funeral home director from Peterborough, Ontario, who had my hat on. We could see that green feather waggling all afternoon. Mom was sitting a couple of rows in front of him wearing a blue blouse (for the Blue Jays), giant round sunglasses, and a big white hat with fake flowers all over it, and eating hot dogs, looking like someone from It's a *Mad, Mad, Mad, Mad, World*. Mr. Kay looked like someone from a Dickens novel or a Vincent Price movie, with a long Roman nose and jet black eyebrows. You could easily picture him wearing a black top hat with a long black sash down the back driving a large black brougham with a casket in the back. When I would tease him about being a funeral director, he would smile, puff his cigarette from the black cigarette holder he always used, and say, "I'll be the last guy to let you down, Jim. The last guy to let you down."

"Maybe, just maybe sir, but with Dorothy Rose around, you've got some serious competition."

A few days later, when she and Willy had gone their separate ways, I found the Rovers tickets in a parcel by the kitchen door, along with a carton of Newport cigarettes, and a pack of Werther's butterscotch candies.

I scalped the tickets and spent the money on books, a couple of sweet restaurant meals by the water, and a bottle of rye.

THE I BEHIND THE I

t is early morning, mid-autumn. I've taken a mug of strong black coffee and some books onto the back deck where it's cool enough to need a sweater. My wife, Rose, sleeps in.

The giant old olive bushes that flank the wooden deck have grown so large they reach several feet above the railings now, and along with a big umbrella and the vine-covered trellises at either end, we enjoy a modicum of shade, shelter, and privacy. Those olive bushes blossom late this time of year and give off a sweet, intoxicating aroma that always has a surprisingly beneficial effect upon my overall peace of mind. When those blossoms fade, however, so too will autumn slip away. There won't be many more mornings like this until sometime next spring, and that realization, of course, brings on a rather light-hearted melancholy which, in turn, triggers a bouquet of random realizations.

It happens to everyone of course, but being in my late fifties, segueing into my early sixties, has brought with it an unanticipated responsibility. Younger people, especially men, are seeking me out with their existential quandaries.

Here on the deck, after fetching a second mug of joe, and finishing the book *Night Train to Lisbon* by Pascal Mercier, I have retrieved Fernando Pessoa's *The Book of Disquiet* from the stack I've brought with me, and dig in where I left off reading eight years ago. I underline shamelessly, and am therefore able to go directly to the passage I want. Pessoa writes, "...I'm like a traveler who suddenly finds himself in a strange town, without knowing how he got there... Suddenly I've woken up in the middle of a bridge, leaning over the river and knowing that I exist more solidly than the person I was up till now."

Mercier begins his novel about the train to Lisbon with an encounter on a bridge. A professor walking to the university one morning interrupts a young woman whom he believes is about to jump off the bridge to her death. She comes to sit in on his class instead and leaves in the middle of it. As he continues his lecture, he watches her through the class-room window, walking away across the campus lawns. This encounter so sparks his imagination that he changes his life forever. That very day he resigns his tenured position, closes up his apartment, drops in on his favorite book vendor, then takes the night train to Lisbon on an existential journey.

Mercier is wise to give a nod to Pessoa in his narrative. The mysterious revolutionary character Prado in *Night Train* leaves behind, when he dies, a manuscript of his own that is pure Pessoa in its investigations of the introspective mind.

And when a mind so investigates itself in this way, I ask myself once more, who is the "I" behind the "I"?

On this gray autumn morning, sitting on the deck before my wife wakes up, it's easy to time travel, carried on the sweet perfume of these olive blossoms into the inner world of per-sonal myth, the manifested self, the one who's always been there.

"You've always been confident in who you are," said Rose last night over a bottle or two of good red wine. We were discussing friends and acquaintances whose one common trait is an underlying insecurity regarding who they perceive themselves to be. I figure I've had to reinvent myself five or six times over the years, and that can be traumatizing in a "shit, here we go again, back to the drawing board" kind of way. But confident about who I am? Well, confidence comes and goes, as does my sense of self- assuredness. On that score, I always felt I was running about par, average, pretty much okay.

But enough about me.

What started us on this topic was a recent visit from a U.K. buddy of ours, Martin. As Rose and I postmortem the week we spent with him, she laughs, "He seems like he's caught in some kind of miserable loop. Everywhere he turns things are going sour on the poor guy. I hope it doesn't turn him into a misery guts." In his early forties, a bit younger than Rose, quite a bit younger than me, Martin finds himself in transition. His job, his love life, his writing, all seem to have become tangled up in blue. He's come to America to get out of the rut he's been in, or as they say, to get himself sorted. He's a brilliant man, a trained actor, a good writer despite his dyslexia, and, when on his home soil, he's the man you want when you feel a good pub crawl coming on. Philosophically, he can go almost anywhere with the right mental lubrication, so this "misery guts" thing is a temporary symptom, not his usual self. Also, he has developed a back problem, and if anything will make you miserable, that'll do it. I blame his job, and his unhealthy alliance with it, for his back pain. Too much tension can get you clenched. Nobody wants to be clenched. And getting de-clenched can be a long and arduous project.

The night before he flew home, after Rose gave up on us and went to bed, Martin and I sat up late, sipping wine and talking, circling about his various troubles like ravens in the moonlight, until it all boiled down to one basic bit of advice.

"Look," I said, "first and foremost, you have an obligation to yourself to be happy. Why? For lots of reasons. But primarily because you're no bloody good to anyone if you're miserable, meaning, not okay with Martin."

"Okay with Martin?"

"Yeah. Happiness is not a self-indulgence. It's a key component to what you bring to the world, and what the world can bring to you. Whatever you need to do to be happy with Martin, get working on it. You'll just make yourself and everyone else around you miserable until you do. Besides, you'll feel better just knowing you're back in charge. Hate your job? Come up with a plan. Take the pressure your job is putting on you—clenching you up—and put that pressure to work motivating you to get the fuck out and take the pressure off. Easier said than done, I'm sure, but how long can you go on like this? Your love life makes you crazy? Table it. Issue some pink slips, stop taking calls or answering emails. Just let it die on the vine. After all, how can you be good for so-and-so if you can't be good for Martin?"

"Would that I could," he replied while heaving a sigh of exasperation, looking more and more hopeless, miserable, and forlorn by the second. He stared into a distant corner of the room that I was certain had his current heartthrob's face hidden in it.

"By the way," I tried to lighten his load, "you should *enjoy* this time between relationships. It won't last long, anyway. You'll fall bass-ackwards into something with someone soon enough. But for now, invest some time in crawling back into your own skin. Hang out with my good pal Martin in the interim. Clearly, he's the one needing attention. You're so tangled up with exigencies, contingencies, and hypotheses, you haven't noticed you're really just suffering from neglect."

"Yes, well, that's the hard part, isn't it?" he replied. "The commitments pile up and the misery quotient grows. It's hard to tell what the bloody hell to do about it."

"Well, all I can tell you is, stop giving a shit about shit you don't give a shit about, and you'll feel a whole lot better pretty soon thereafter. The whole wide world is dying to tell you how to cope with it. A woman who's interested will tell you how to make love to her, or how not to, if you can shut up long enough to listen to her. An employer will tell you what they want to hear about you. My point is, get okay with Martin and the rest of the world will probably get okay with Martin, too."

"So, what is to be done?" Martin bravely asks the question of the ages.

"Beats me," I reply. "But here's the hard part, and this I learned the hardest way, when I was a younger man and saw roadblocks at every turn. If it's art you want to make, either through your acting, your writing, or whatever means you choose to express yourself, keep this one thing foremost in your mind; *anyone* who suggests that you *not* make your art, I don't care if it's a best friend, a lover, a mom or dad, *anyone* who wants to impose on you a priority that takes you away from your work for whatever reason—*that person is not your friend.* And they're gonna have to go."

Now, this rudimentary bit of amateur psychology won't work for people with big problems, but it can help to maybe overcome the average everyday variety. Especially if those troubles have been piling up earning compound interest on your soul. Anything beyond this is above my pay scale and I'm, quite frankly, not qualified to venture one step further than my own personal experiences. But hey, I've been around.

There is an echo of Pessoa in these musings from someone's personal netherworld. In *Night Train to Lisbon*, the Pessoa-inspired Prado character gives a similar reality check to the one above. "Disappointment," says the character Prado, "is considered bad. A thoughtless prejudice. How, if not through disappointment, should we discover what we have expected and hoped for? And where, if not in this discovery, should self-knowledge lie? So, how could one gain clarity about oneself without disappointment?"

And I'm thinking, what if the "I" mentioned earlier, is acting out a role, or minding its own business, so to speak, and a second inner "I" is watching? That the second "I" can be astonished by how unpremeditated and random the actions of the outer "I" really are should come as no surprise. I would simply explain this as a division of labor between outer and inner personas, outer and inner selves. Think of one as operating on impulse power; the second has a hyperdrive. We humans like to move about on impulse power because we need to get things done to maintain ourselves, get food, go to a job, and so on. But if I focus on my impulse-driven self too much, I might miss the smell of these late autumn's olive flowers. And that's not why I'm here.

Important things are now happening every day. Yesterday, Rose had a chat with a real estate agent in Oxford, England. We may be able to rent a little house near Jessica Payne. That would allay one of my biggest worries about our intended stay there next winter/spring. Jessica and Rose are close, and Jessica loves a good project. Right now, we're it. She's one of those apparitions who, when her eyes meet yours, makes you fall in love all over again with the world.

Last night our old chum Larry Carlisle came by for a few drinks. In a couple of days he goes in for prostate cancer surgery. He's embraced his situation and is going forward with brave commitment. Lean, clear minded, and true. Some expert doctors think it's a disease that, if not aggressive, should go untreated. His appears to be unaggressive. He's going in anyway. I really admire him.

Here on the deck, birds chatter hilariously up in the trees as though they had gathered for a mid-morning tea. Most leaves are down. The ones that remain are a dazzling yellow or a fading shade of green. The gray overcast of the sky makes the fall colors pop, and the aroma of the olive flowers can lift one into a blissful state of contemplation, but in a few minutes, I'll rise and go upstairs to my writing room. I will file away the huge stacks of bills and receipts and crap that have been piling up, finish tidying my office, roust Rose, who has been sleeping in after a long week of editing, and get myself back to work.

A week or so after Martin's return to England he leaves a happy message on our voicemail. "All is well, job on hold, bad girlfriend out the door, the back is on the mend, oh, and please tell Jimmy, that Martin has taken his advice. Martin is okay as long as he's fine—with Jimmy."

Somewhere a few blocks from here an ambulance siren sounds, and when it does, all the birds stop their chattering, and listen.

Do Conservatives Dream of an Electric Jesus?

I must admit I'm sick and tired of the apocalypse.

Looking around, at contemporary culture, for as long as I can remember, there has been an ever-growing subgenre of science fiction books, movies, TV, graphic novels, etc., regarding the apocalypse, or worse, the post-apocalypse. I, for one, find it off-putting. Always have. I don't endorse or want to participate in the end of the world. I don't find it romantic, or entertaining, or stylistically pleasing, and I wouldn't give two shits for the mythic superstition that spawned the idea in the first place. And yet here we are, in a *Blade Runner* world where everyone is sick, everything's broken, and nobody cares.

Since the 1950s there have been tons of media with either an apocalyptic or post-apocalyptic theme. Putting a number to this is hard to calculate because the subject is category defiant, blending and bleeding into various subcategories. There are the dystopian films, like *Blade Runner*. There are the films about Armageddon, the actual event of world ending minus the how or why, all with the implied excuse that this is predestined, which cheerily excuses us from responsibility for the destruction of the Earth or the responsibility to do anything to stop it. Movies like *The Day After Tomorrow, 2012, The End of the World,* for those excited or titillated by catastrophe, novels, television series, radio plays from the good old days, on and on, are all in great supply. One could argue further that our contemporary culture is underpinned with this dangerous notion that the end of the world is nigh, that there is nothing we can do about it, and that it is somehow *sexy.*

One depressing, almost subliminal, side effect of this genre of apocalypse is the insidious notion of its inevitability. Climate change, racial inequality, wealth disparity, gun violence, on and on. We can't seem to get anywhere on these problems by voting. In fact, wealthy elites everywhere are fed up with letting people vote at all, and doing all they can to prevent it. A New Feudalism is dawning, and it is right at our door.

And don't get me started on Zombies. More about them later.

The movie *Blade Runner,* now enjoying its fortieth anniversary, is, as everyone knows, based on the Philip K. Dick novel *Do Androids Dream of Electric Sheep?* In it, the one percent, as we have come to call the super-rich, have fled the polluted, corrupt, and dying planet Earth for a newly discovered, and presumably conquered, more pristine, celestial world elsewhere. Those humans who are left behind are sick from radiation poisoning and, because of it, have all but stopped reproducing. They must fend for themselves amid the hard rain and lack of necessities—first and foremost, the comfort and companionship of other living beings, specifically, our fellow mammals. So, if you can afford it, you can buy a "replicant" goat, or dog, cat, horse, even a sheep.

Those humans who have yet to be infected are given as an incentive to emigrate an "organic android" as a personal slave. But some of those human replicants malfunction and go rogue. In the book as well as the film, the character Rick Deckar is a bounty hunter of these malfunctioning robots. To these he gives an empathy test that no replicant can pass, and when they fail, he terminates them.

Harrison Ford, at the time the picture came out in 1982, was high in the footsteps of Humphrey Bogart and Steve McQueen as America's Cool-But-Star-Crossed-Tough-Guy film star. He was fresh from mega movie series hits *Star Wars* and *Indiana Jones*. In *Blade Runner* he has a love interest in Sean Young, playing a female replicant who reminds every guy of the crazy-chic, sex-freak, long lost weekend he says he'd rather forget, but always puts a wicked smile on his face.

It is useful to point out here that in the original *Star Wars* trilogy of films, the Evil Empire is defeated by the patriots of the Old Republic, or the Rebellion. Indiana Jones, the adventuring archeologist cum university professor (imagine, a college professor as action hero?), succeeds in recovering historic artifacts that contain keys to ancient mysticisms, mysteries, and magic.

Apocalyptic and post-apocalyptic fiction cannot end triumphantly or even happily. There is no longer the noble ambition of saving the world; the best we can do is survive it. But we do apparently get some gear; sleeveless leather jackets, boots, lots and lots of motorcycles, and the omnipresent and never-ending supply of guns and ammo. Really cool, huh?

In *Blade Runner*, World War Terminus has happened, and no one knows any longer why it was fought, or by whom, or even who won. *Blade Runner* ends with the romance between the Ford character, Rick Deckar, and his hot girl replicant heading for the hills to find a little happiness, knowing their affair has an expiration date when her battery runs out. There are many director's cuts with different endings, but that's the one I remember seeing when the film was first released.

The film's producers wanted Dick to write a book treatment of the film and offered him a lot of money to do so, but to the author's everlasting credit, he steadfastly refused, insisting they bring back the original *Do Androids Dream of Electric Sheep?* instead. This was a stroke of genius on his part as the film's worldwide success ensured that his entire catalogue was eventually put back in print, garnering him millions of new fans hungry for good sci-fi as a result. But the author died shortly before the film's release, and therefore never enjoyed the fame and fortune that was his due.

Recently, close viewers of the original film think they have uncovered the film's long-lost secret, that Rick Deckar was himself a replicant. In the book, the Deckar character certainly is human and, unbeknownst to himself and to all around him, is slowly becoming a "chickenhead," sliding into an enfeebling mental illness from radiation exposure.

Apocalyptic, post-apocalyptic, dystopian films and books have been in vogue for a long time, especially since the Cold War nuclear bomb scare of the 1940s, '50s, and '60s. But it hardly started there.

For hundreds of years, legions of religious fanatics, particularly Evangelicals, have clung to the same lunatic scenario that gains easy traction with contemporary chickenheads, idiots, the illiteratti, and power-mongers the world over. It goes like this: Jesus is coming back, the book of John at the end of the Bible tells us so. He's going to choose who's been naughty and nice, pick the nice ones, and they'll live in happy

happy joy joy for (only) a thousand years. Then it's right on up to heaven with the lot of them.

Certain of these people, being ignorant, and so in awe at their own nascent cognitive abilities, found it easy to believe that, if *they* only believed hard enough, *they* could be the chosen ones. In effect, *they* could force the Lord's hand. So, *they* came up with the ingenious interpretation of this old book of horror stories that if *they* could only bring about the end of the world *themselves*, that would make Jesus really really happy, and he'll come back sooner than planned to reward *them* for their great devotion and faith. And those Evangelicals are so special, by virtue of their Evangelicalism, that they get to go home with Jesus, and no one else can come along. Because they're so special, they get to be the last persons on Earth. And aren't they fortunate to be so special.

In America, this nonsense began in the 1730s when a nut job named George Whitefield came over from England and crisscrossed American rural communities proclaiming "The Great Awakening." His nonsense wouldn't go over in more educated British locales, but out where the corn grew tall, and where reading and writing were not considered a virtue, followers would buy into his old-fashioned Calvinist rhetoric of fire and brimstone. Many listened with a wild-eyed frenzy of belief, and their numbers grew. So numerous were they that patriots courted them to support the colonies' break with England. Eventually, the Evangelicals came to endorse the American Revolution. Why? Because a fight between the greatest power on Earth, England, and the upstart colonies would bring about the Apocalypse.

A hundred and ninety-one years later, measuring from the ratification of the U.S. Constitution to the election of Ronald Reagan as president, these dangerously stupid people were back again and began to take over the American government, and their plan of destroying the Earth for Jesus gained serious traction.

It was Ronald Reagan who gave the Evangelicals their biggest boost, reopening a door a previous generation had thought it sealed shut forever, when he stood outside a bombed abortion clinic and said, "I don't agree [with bombing abortion clinics], but I understand."

James Watt, President Reagan's first Secretary of the Interior, when asked to justify despoiling our natural heritage via oil drilling, mining, and the selling off of public national park lands, simply said matter-of-factly that the end of the world was nigh upon us, so who cares?

When President George W. Bush was asked why he wasn't concerned about climate change, he shrugged his shoulders and said, "We'll all be dead by then anyway, so who cares?" It was the first time I could remember a president proclaiming indifference to the survival of those who come after us. The greatest criminals in human history will be those who stood in the way of preventing climate change.

The very notion of a "republic"—a system of government where citizens elect representatives to vote their wishes and concerns into laws that govern society rather than having power concentrated in the person of a single despot, or warlord, or a cabal of elites—was at one time a utopian ideal. Thomas Paine, according to scholar Eric Foner, "helped to create and publicize the new secular ideas of human progress and perfectibility which emerged in the 18th century."

The Perfectibility of Man, the Dignity of Man. I've been missing these concepts in the underpinning themes that drive Western discourse and expression over the last few decades. And, certainly, there is no room in apocalyptic lore for entertaining any such notions. Odd, is it not, that people who get excited about the corruptibility of man refute the opposite? I mean, if man is corruptible, he sure as hell must be perfectible.

I guess what I'm advocating here is the Return of the Ideal.

Without humanity's focus on striving with an ideal as our guide, we are metaphysically rudderless. Once religion outlived its usefulness, it was to be replaced with Reason, but Reason proved to be heartless, and I feel civilization foundering on misdirected abstractions, e.g., "But Jefferson owned slaves," is the rhetorical equivalent of "...but Hillary's emails"— in the sense that because Thomas Jefferson owned slaves, the ideal he postulated, that "all men are created equal," is somehow negated, hypocritical, and therefore false. Ritchie Robertson, in his brilliant tome *The Enlightenment: The Pursuit of Happiness 1680–1790*, suggests we have become victims of "presentism—that is, a tendency to see the past only from a present-day perspective, and to ignore or underestimate its difference from the present." And because of that presentism, respect for the constitution has plummeted without rebuke. Just as, since we didn't know the content of Hillary Clinton's personal emails, all her progressive notions about suffrage and self-government should be discounted—resulting in people, who have no education regarding our constitution and its place in history, getting elected to public office with the sole intent of destroying the contract. And voilà! Donald Trump becomes president.

In the *Blade Runner* world, the idea of extinction is, dare I say it, cool: because we're so special, we get to be the last persons on Earth.

Meanwhile, Zombies, living happily as decomposing cannibals, are, along with our virtual destruction, accepted and popular. Why? Because killing without conscience is fun, and any one group we don't like can be zombified, so it's perfectly okay to get rid of them. So having no respect for the future leaves us no respect for the dead either. In a similar way, Deckar's affection for his emotionally inert replicant affords the possibility of sex without consequences. Killing without conscience, sex without consequences. Every script writer's dream.

At the root of it all of course is the propaganda of helplessness. Climate change? Sorry, nothing we can do. Perpetual warfare? War will always be with us. The fat book of stupid horrors, the Bible, tells us so. The Bible is a great source for much of this nonsense—such as the poor will always be with us (Deuteronomy 15:11). If that's the case, we can't, and really shouldn't, help them; how convenient—for the rich.

U.S. representatives have said several times on the floor of Congress that Noah's great rainbow is proof that God promised to never again destroy the world by flood, therefore climate science must be wrong.

Do conservatives dream of an electric Jesus? Of course they do. Because conservatism is not a philosophy. It is dogma. It doesn't evolve, change, or seek intellectual improvement because it cannot. Why? Because conservatism is a mere rationalization against the notion that with wealth comes social responsibility. Why? Because the hoarding of wealth denudes society of the resources needed to fix what is broken, to invent solutions to unanticipated problems. To heal itself.

I jotted down a note to myself back in 2014 when a writer in a *New York Times* interview was asked what book remains unwritten. The writer's answer was profound—the sequel to *1984*, where Big Brother is exposed and defeated. Somebody should get to work on that. Come to think of it, a *Star Wars* series where the Empire is brought down once and for all would be enjoyable as well. Remember, in the *Star Trek* universe we begin *after* climate change, perpetual war, and hopeless poverty have all been eradicated, so humans can set out upon what should be their true destiny—humanism.

Meanwhile, it appears that the only fictional hero who really wants to save the world is Dr. Who. He's a Time Lord and, unfortunately, the last one. Isn't it about time the rest of us rolled up our sleeves and gave it one more try?

DIGBY AT THE SWAN

Here in the Lake District, it's either raining, about to rain, or just finished raining. —Cab driver, Grasmere, England

Around us the hills are tall, steep, woolly, and close. Big nature in most of Europe is always close-in. On top of you, so to speak. Here, the descriptions in Wordsworth's poems are still near exact. Through pure coincidence it is the season of daffodils. In Oxford the other day, a friend of ours began reciting by heart, as she walked us around the grounds of the great university:

> I wandered lonely as a cloud
> That floats on high o'er vales and hills,
> When all at once I saw a crowd,
> A host, of golden daffodils;
> Beside the lake, beneath the trees,
> Fluttering and dancing in the breeze...

And it's true, you come upon them, unexpectedly, in glorious clusters. In this environment of gray clouds and forest green fens, sudden bursts of primary colors are something to rejoice over. The buildings nearby have walls of stone or white plaster, often cracked. The stones in the pasture fences and the ancient houses are a very dark gray. The roads that turn and bend are narrow, the fields a springtime baby green.

And yes, it is raining. The kind of soft velvet rain I want to run naked in.

The Swan Hotel, mentioned in Wordsworth's 1805 poem "The Waggoner," was built in 1650. As a North American, just staying at an inn that is over three hundred and fifty years old is exceedingly cool. Patrons at the pub in the Swan Hotel are polite and for the most part keep to themselves, but some are openly friendly, and respond to our enthusiasms with a cheerful willingness to share their knowledge of the area. My wife, Rose, and I find them charming and helpful.

And then there are the dogs.

Pub dogs are a real thing in this district. Always well-behaved and dutiful as they patrol the perimeters, lapping up errant bits of pub fare that fall from plates, or are brushed from tables and laps, shaken from napkins. Like most local pubs, the one at the Swan Hotel has a separate entrance for travelers on foot, locals with their muddy boots, raincoats, and, of course, big wet dogs.

This pub is small, but roomy enough to provide a step down to the dog walkers' room, where there are pegs for hanging hats, coats, and leashes (leads). There's a small fireplace to melt away the chill of rainy weather. Better than cozy. If you ever dreamed of a place to take a good book, a journal, and time to while away an afternoon, this is it.

Grasmere itself is a little village just across the Keswick Road, a one-minute walk. Over a stone bridge, down the street, and around a corner is another pub, and a small sign at the side entrance reads, "Only Good Dogs Allowed." Rose and I decide the reason that sign is there must have been one very bad dog. But the terrain all around screams dog heaven. If I owned a dog, it could only be in a place like this, where it could gallop along at its own pace, gleefully sniffing out the leavings of countless pooches who came before, and pubs that allow only good dogs.

The Swan Hotel has been here since long before Wordsworth's time. The stairs are narrow and creaky, and the place, like so much of England, has a comforting sense of permanence and warmth that embraces and welcomes as you step in from the chilling rain. There's a four-star hotel in town, tucked imperceptibly in among the stone bridge and other small buildings, and although we ate there once during our stay, the thought of staying there instead of the Swan never occurred to us. The Swan is what we came for, and it's taken a lifetime to get here.

In high school I had a pocket-sized fat little hardback copy of Wordsworth's poems. Not only has it survived over forty-nine years, but its pale blue dust jacket has remarkably little wear and tear. This because I've never scribbled on the pages, no underlines, no folded corners. Not even any coffee stains. It fits neatly into a sports coat pocket and has been a trusted companion on many a sojourn hither and yon. In younger days I would skip school and go for walks along the C&O Canal, not far from my girlfriend's house, and find a sunny glade where I could read, listen to the water, sniff the spring or autumn breezes, cogitate, and maybe scribble a line or two of my own.

I used to wonder as I read those lush, flowing, pastoral lines, if these Lake Poets knew, or had some inkling, that the Industrial Age would spoil so much of the natural wonders they held so dear. If the paeans they were writing to the flora and fauna all around them were elegiac, a farewell to Eden itself? On some level, I believe they were.

A two- or three-mile walk down Keswick Road from the Swan is Dove Cottage, Wordsworth's home, and next to that the Wordsworth Trust Museum. The hotel clerk asks if we like to walk, and, of course, we do. He suggests we walk there and back, but after she thinks about it, Rose suggests we cab to the museum and walk back.

At Dove Cottage, a young woman, late twenties, tallish, quiet, is giving visitors the tour. She shows guests around with a prepared monologue about the famous poet and his life-style, with anecdotes about Samuel Taylor Coleridge's many visits. She reminds me of many young women I knew in high school and college, a young starry-eyed romantic, nervous and halting. As she struggles to be heard, only her passion for the place forces her to erupt with information about this couch, or that chair. She is here because she has been smitten by the Lake Poets and the legends they left behind. Clearly, she has found her proper place in the world. The bed where the poet slept is narrow, and tilted a little like a deck chair, because he had digestion issues and needed to sleep partially sitting up.

Rose is a poet, well-known in certain circles in the States, with more than a few fans in the U.K. as well. I am, as a writer, doubly blessed because my wife, Rose Solari, aside from being a superb poet, playwright, novelist, and educator, is also a terrific editor. (These lines you're reading now have her magic dust all over them.) She has written ahead to the Wordsworth Trust Museum to introduce herself and let them know we're coming to visit. Their curator meets us at the door. He escorts us to the coffee shop where we are joined by the Literary Director, and after a bite and a bit of coffee, we take a turn through the public museum, which, unexpectedly leads us to The Vault, which is not open to the public.

Rose and I are pleasantly stunned. The Vault is a climate-controlled softly lit chamber, soundproof, still. After a few minutes explaining the needs and difficulties of historic preservation, our host, the curator, opens a drawer and takes out Dorothy Wordsworth's own personal commonplace book written very legibly in her own hand, and he invites me to turn the pages and give it a read, as he and Rose get acquainted chatting about the museum's involvement in the local poetry community.

As I gently turn the pages of Dorothy's book (I can't believe he's letting me touch it), he points out a discrepancy in the dates she has inscribed and a poem she was working on that he originally found pasted into the back of a book belonging to one of her friends.

While referring to her "odd dates" a quote from Dorothy; "It is now April 6th, 3 years since my illness began." The curator points out that scholarship does not agree with Dorothy's timeline here.

Rose points out that Dorothy may have been willfully deceptive, and like any good pedagogue, Rose can cite instances. I suggest they compare Dorothy's more suspicious dates with other correspondences of hers and her intimates. He leads me across the room to shelves lined with rows of volumes of Wordsworth's collected letters, and we spend several minutes reading letters to and from written at and around that time period. Nothing.

Then, he refers to a famous visit that young John Keats made to Rydal Mount, a larger house nearby where Wordsworth spent his last two years, to find the Wordsworths not at home. Keats waited a short while for them to return, and when they didn't, he told the housekeeper, "I left a note behind Dorothy's portrait." The note was never found. "Perhaps he didn't mean a portrait of Dorothy, but a portrait belonging to her," I suggest. The curator furrows his brow and says "no, no, no, it is generally agreed he meant a portrait of Dorothy." But the whole thing is so intriguing, it's hard not to get caught up in a mystery that is some two hundred and sixty years old. As we're leaving the chamber, I good-naturedly quote Sherlock Holmes, "You know, once you have eliminated the obvious, whatever remains, however improbable, must be the truth."

I'll confess, I don't know the English well enough to tell when I'm being impertinent, so I try damn hard not to be. He's not impressed, but I hope he's amused.

I thought we were leaving, but no, he now guides us into the Deep Vault. There, he produces another of Dorothy's diaries, where, in the back, Wordsworth himself had scribbled the opening lines to "The Prelude."

> —Was it for this
> That one, the fairest of all rivers, lov'd
> To blend his murmurs with my Nurse's song,

It's enough to make a poetry lover's knees go weak. Rose and the curator and the literary expert discuss the Wordsworth Trust's various reading series and another program that offers a yearlong writer in residence post—*a year in Grasmere?!?* She has also been picking poetic brains about a theme she's been researching regarding the break between American and British poets after WWII. I can listen to this kind of next-level chatter all day.

The walk back to the Swan seemed to take forever, and in the middle of a short climb over a large fen, it started to rain.

Now, when an English person asks if you like to walk, be wary; they don't necessarily mean a casual stroll say, around the corner or some such. They mean a vigorous long forced march over rough terrain, hill and dale, in any and all weather, and now here we are, trudging along the top of a fen, lugging bags of books, notes, and loot purchased at the museum gift shop, plus more swag our hosts had gifted us, with the hotel nowhere in sight. Should we walk back to the museum? Should we soldier on? The bags are getting wet. The books are getting heavy—worse, our precious journals and books are in danger of getting soaked along with the two of us. Not good.

Just as we're beginning to dither, a couple comes strolling down a path to the road from the top of the hill. They are on a driving tour of the Lake District and had pulled over to hike up the hill and back. Their car is parked right nearby. It only takes a moment for them to ascertain our dilemma and offer to give us a lift. In the car, the four of us laugh about the distances on maps being so close but the reality of travel taking so long.

As Rose and I stumble into the hotel, she thinks it a good idea that I should run back out and flag them down and try to invite them to come in for a drink and hang out for a while, maybe even spring for supper. The clerk is standing behind the desk with our keys. "They said they were on a tight schedule," I say, "they obviously have plans."

"So what? Run out there and ask, they might change their plans."

"But, they've got to be gone by now."

"Well run out and see," she says, "hurry!"

"Are we having an argument?" the clerk interrupts, his eyes lit up and ready for a show.

"Of course not."

"You two got caught in the rain, and now you're arguing?"

"No, no, we're not arguing, we're not, we're, we're married, that's all."

For some reason, from that moment on, the staff at the hotel will refer to us as "you two."

"So, what are you two up to today then?"

"No arguing today, you two."
"Will you two be back for lunch?"

The restaurant at the Swan is charming, the food excellent. Rose and I are great talkers who never run out of fascinating topics to explore, and this trip has afforded so much material we feel we'll never be caught up. At dinner we are babbling on and on about the museum, Dove Cottage, the couple on the fen, when we both realize at the same instant that, although there isn't an empty seat in the place, everyone else is dead silent, heads bowed, as they eat, cleaning their plates with exactitude and efficiency, while Rose and I are yakking up a storm, quaffing before, during, and after dinner beverages all the while.

The next morning at the reception desk to drop off our key, I will remark to the clerk, "Last night at supper, you could have heard a pin drop in there. Are most people in England abused at the dinner table as children?"

"Hmm," he ponders sincerely, mulling it over. "I've never thought of it before, but yes, I guess you could say, yes we were." A young woman co-worker joins him behind the desk, and he inquires, "Does your family talk at all during mealtime?"

"Nary a peep, we're all too busy eating," she smiles, then trots off on another chore. Of course, Rose and I will talk about it all during lunch.

On a stroll about town, one shop has a hat rack on the sidewalk. Rain hats for women. I insist Rose buy one. She has big hair. She often laments that her hair does "the horizontal dance of humiliation" in humid or wet weather. I think it looks terrific, can't get big enough for me, but I can see the damage it's done to her psyche. I pick out a rain hat for her and suggest strongly she buy it.

"He says I have to buy this," she informs the shopkeeper, as though it were a penance.

Later, back at the Swan, we're in the pub, discussing the odd dining habits and wet weather gear of folks in this part of the world, when a couple enters the pub trailing a large dog with black curly hair and a big snout, shaggy, moist from the rain, but clearly very pleased to be entering a warm congenial atmosphere with fresh-cooked flavors in the air. They take a booth catty-corner to ours and the dog crouches down under the table, then turns a half circle so he can lie down looking out into the room.

He looks at me and his tongue drops out in a friendly pant. I smile.

He withdraws his tongue and nods his head, rather like in recognition, one mammal to another, kind of guy to guy.

Rose is talking.

As we chat, a man enters. His wife is back in their room. They are dining in, on their honeymoon. He says she wants a bottle of champagne.

Two or three women at other tables catch a clue, and almost in unison start saying to their male companions, "Hey big spender, where's *my* bubbly?"

"*I'd* like some champers!" another chimes in.

Corks are now popping all around the room.

My lunch arrives. Fish and chips, the chips meaning French fries. Delicious. We stay away from the bubbly. I love English pub ales and bitters, Rose prefers German beer. Every so often I feel someone looking at me. It's the big scruffy pooch under yonder table. He lifts his head when we make eye contact, gives a pant, then rests his head back down on his paws, which are resting one atop the other under his chin.

A tartar sauce–slathered French fry slips from my fingers and hits the floor.

"Are you going to get that?" I hear, clear as a bell.

I look around, Rose is talking about possibly spending a year here at the residency program at the Wordsworth Trust.

"Seriously, are you going to get it?"

I look up and see the dog under the table staring at me intently. When our eyes meet, his eyes drop down to look at the French fry on the floor. Then back at me.

"You mean the French fry?" I think back at him.

"Yes, the chip, are you going to get that or what?"

"It's dirty."

"No, it's not, and if you're not going to get it I will."

We both look down at the French fry and then back at each other.

"You can have it," I think back.

"Really?"

"I said so, didn't I?"

"Yes, but if I haul myself up and come over there and then you pick it up, that would be a cruel thing to do." I was indeed thinking of picking it up, but only as to not leave it there on the floor. He starts to get up, then thinks better of it. "My people will think I'm misbehaving if I get up and come over there for no reason. They'll think I'm begging from a stranger."

"Oh, for Christ's sake, come and get it!"

Am I arguing telepathically with a dog?

"We aren't arguing, we made a deal." He's on his feet and easing out from under the table. His people hardly notice, enjoying champagne with their fish and chips.

He strolls over, nonchalant, and when he gets to the table, I hear, "Last chance."

"Go ahead, take it," I laugh. He sits down, then leans forward and laps up the chip. Panting happily after swallowing it whole. I feed him a couple more.

"You're so good with animals," my wife compliments me, then returns to the topic at hand.

The pooch looks over to his people, who are smiling back at us. I smile at them. "Does this happen often?" I'm thinking.

"Not often enough," he says. I give him another chip.

I pet him on the head for a minute. He sits quietly enjoying the attention, licking his chops. I scratch behind his big ears, the back of his head, petting him gently on the back. His fur is like silk. When he thinks that's enough, he politely gets up to return to his table, turns to look at me, and says, "Thanks, that was great."

"Want some more? I can't eat them all."

"I better not, but thanks again."

He strolls back, crouches to get under the table, then curls around to rest his chin on his paws crossed at the wrists.

Later in our room, I say, "That dog was really talking to me. Has that ever happened to you?"

"Of course it has," and Rose's off on a lengthy discourse of her long and storied relationship with her old pooch who passed on way before we met.

The next day we're strolling through Grasmere, when I feel a familiar presence, and looking across the street, I see a woman standing on the corner talking with a friend, and there beside her is one of those black and white herding dogs, looking at me so curiously. I tried thinking at him, "Hey buddy!" He looks startled, and turns instantly aside looking somewhere else, quite deliberately ignoring me, shifting his weight uncomfortably. Then I get a sneaky little side-eyed glance to check if I'm still there, and a nervous twitch when he discovers that I am.

I'm rather wounded.

A few steps later a couple of older gents are walking their hounds; nothing.

A car glides by and a small white dog with his paws on the windowsill is looking at me with a curious cocked head, turning his head to keep eye contact as they slowly roll past.

"Hey there," I think at him.

"Hey there, got any treats?" I get back.

At the Only Good Dogs pub, a pooch was lapping up water from a bowl on the front step, and as we walked by, he looked up at me, his muzzle dripping. Neither of us could think of anything to say.

Just then a familiar voice sounded in my head.

"There you are, hey."

It was him!

The same couple from the Swan Pub the day before came strolling up, with their big curly black dog on a lead.

Rose greeted them cordially, but I approached the beast, got down on one knee, and he gave my cheek a big wet lick as I playfully rubbed him about the ears. He put a paw on my shoulder, enjoying the attention.

"There's my pal," I laughed.

"Pal!" I heard in my head.

"What kind of dog is he?" Rose asks.

"He's a Labradoodle, a new mixed breed, half poodle, half Labrador."

"Brilliant idea," I say. "Labs are a bit dozy, and poodles can be hyper but very intelligent."

"Oh, he's a smart one, yes he is. And cool as a cucumber."

"And what's his name?"

"The name is Digby."

Did the dog say that, or his owners, or all three? The name echoes in my head.

"Digby Digby Digby!" he answers back, and puts his paw up once more. I give it a shake.

"Digby, my buddy!" I laugh as he gives my face another wet lick. We hug.

When I stand back up, he bumps his shoulder on my knee, sits down at my side, and chills with me while everyone talks, looking up from time to time to encourage more pets and scratches.

Some days later, as we're checking out, another couple is leaving as well. One of them has an adorable small dog. The man takes it from the wife as she deals with the clerk, and Rose must spend a moment coo-cooing with the pooch. The guy holding the wriggling squealing beasty says to me, "A hundred quid for it then? I'll throw in the lead!?" Rose actually stops to consider as I hustle her out the door.

Back at home a week later, I take an unscientific survey of my pet owner friends. Do you and your pet communicate telepathically? Without having to consider, they universally shoot back that, of course, we do! Any attempt to differentiate the karmic relationships mammals enjoy, and the actual hearing of voices, isn't possible. And I am left to consider:

Digby.

Digby.

Digby.

The Band That Time Forgot

Liner notes for the double album Then and Now by the North Star Band

1976-1982: Return with us now to those thrilling days of yesteryear, when the horrors of late '70s disco and the ravages of early punk rock had left hard-core music fans stranded. When long-haired freaky people still roamed the Earth, an endangered species. At a time when country music's traditional forms had grown stale, and rock had lost its roll, country rockers stepped in to fill the void. Some were outlaws, some were hippies, but all were keepers of the flame of authenticity, and when they came together, the heavens opened up!

Look, up in the sky, it's not Elton, it's not Travolta... It's *The North Star Band!*

Polaris, the North Star, has always guided ships at sea, runaways, and night travelers, steering lost wanderers toward new shorelines and safe havens, and providing a beacon for kindred spirits. Times will change, but the North Star shines on through it all, and with the release of *Then and Now*, we see that one thing remains constant in the crazy mixed-up confusion we call life on Earth. MUSIC!

2022: Bringing blazing guitars, searing pedal steel, a pounding beat of thunder, and three-part howling harmonies to drive hearts into an eighty-beats-per-minute ecstasy of fun, these guys have kept the fires burning.

Five—count 'em, FIVE—accomplished songwriters in one band. Led by rhythm guitarist Al Johnson, a wayward vagabond from Georgetown Law, and four-time Emmy Award–winning bassist Jim Robeson, along with East Coast guitar phenom Gantt Mann Kushner, the wizardry of Jay Jessup's sweet pedal steel (plus mandolin, electric guitar, and banjo), Lou Hager's soulful honky-tonk piano, and Dave Besley's thumping bass riffs, all driven home by the insane poundings of Paul Goldstein's flawless beat. The North Star Band returns our hearts and souls to the epicenter of a place that was once known as Kick-Ass Country!

THEN: Four decades ago, NSB fans piled into dance halls and honky-tonks across the country to hear them play their original music. In venues long faded to dust—Desperados, the Lone Star Cafe, the Carolina Oprey House, County Line, Exit Inn, 117 South Main, and more—they played more than three hundred nights a year. Lou, with his soulful ballads of love and loss, Jimmy with his velvety voice, Dave with his rich vocals and incredible story songs, Al, with his off-beat takes on rednecks, hippies, and Wild Turkey, and Paul with his soul-searching laments, offered fans a band of colors. Records were vinyl and spun at 45 and 33 rpms.

It was Jimmy Carter's Washington, D.C., a lodestar in and of itself. There, for a diamond-like moment, it was okay for the South to meet and shake its ass with the North. Fancy French restaurants became beer-soaked honky-tonks. Office workers stayed out late and called in sick the next day. Ears were ringing and everyone was singing!

The NSB recorded their third album in the summer of 1982, but it was never released. A recession, hard times, and life's imperatives intervened. *Then* is here remastered and ready to be heard for the first time.

NOW: Fast-forward forty years. A reunion show to a packed house at the Birchmere in Alexandria, Virginia, gave birth to *Now*, a collection of new material proving that talent really doesn't fade but always forges new paths.

A tip of the hat is due to other players who passed through this band, legends in their own right: Danny Gatton, Steuart Smith, Mike Melchione, Jim (Ratzo) Silman, Chad Bruce, Johnny Castle, and more.

Yes, the Earth has turned since those days, and yes, the times have changed, but with the release of *Then and Now*, you'll hear continuity, the feeling is the same, and perhaps that alone can help restore some faith in the way things ought to be.

I know, I was there. And miraculously, we're still here.

THROWING IN THE TAO

HENRY MILLER AS LIFE COACH, LITERARY INSTRUCTOR, AND SPIRITUAL GUIDE

t happened somewhere in Minnesota, on Highway 94, a few short decades ago, in the dead of winter. My music partner and I were driving across the Upper Midwest, going from one local college to another, playing music and earning a living. Our first album had, miraculously, sold seventy thousand copies, and we were pretty happy with ourselves. It hadn't come easily though. First, we pressed up a vanity single of a song we had written, then we sent it out to several hundred college and commercial radio stations, then, lo and behold, it got tons of play. Then we petitioned an import-export record label to press it up on an album. Of, course we had blown any money we had on the record we released ourselves, and when the label wanted to do an album, all we had was a collection of demo tapes. We gave them those.

All of this took the better part of a couple of years, and we paid for it all with gig money, out of our pockets, which were always less than half empty. We were aided by the fact that, back then, radio stations could still hire disc jockeys who would play what they pleased. Imagine that. Anyway, because of our little success we were able to bust out of our local market, the Washington, D.C., area, and charge a lot more money for our performances. But with that new inflow there was a corresponding outflow in the form of overhead and time spent hauling our scraggly selves from place to place. The uptick in income was more than consumed by the gross expenditures it took to get us on the road and keep us there. Not to mention the fact that we did all our own booking and promotions as well, backed by the paltry sums we had left. Is this life sounding glamorous yet? In fact, it was a bloody nightmare.

So, there we were, traveling through the frozen north to take our dog-and-pony show to people who would pay for it: universities, colleges, music venues, and bars, which, on this particular junket, were scattered hither and yon across the Upper Midwest.

As I said, it was somewhere on a frozen blue highway in Minnesota that we stopped to use a payphone to check in with the office back home. (Cell phones then were big clunky things that, once you were out of range of your hometown tower, didn't work.) That's when our manager let us know that the label we were with had just told him that we'd have to sue them to get the money they owed us. They were even so bold as to say out loud that it would probably cost us as much as they owed us to get it out of them. The capital up front to get that done we just didn't have. We thought we were sunk.

But we weren't sunk. There was always a milk crate full of books in our traveling van, and on this trip, there was a new favorite. New Directions had just published *The Durrell-Miller Letters, 1935–80*.

We had been listening, on this trip, to Brooklyn-born actor Martin Balsam reading Henry Miller's *Tropic of Cancer* on tape. Man, oh man, Balsam could bring it, with just the right amount of grizzle in his voice, plus that sardonic "everyone's out to fuck us, and who gives a shit," tone that is absolutely unique to a certain generation of Brooklyn-born folks. I swear, for a while, Brooklyn spawned its own genus of human being. Balsam was so authentic, in fact, his thick accent, his attitude, that most people thought it was Henry himself on tape. My partner, Alvis, was also from Brooklyn. He and I were so engrossed in Balsam's performance that we entertained the notion of finding Balsam's agent and hiring him to read our favorite Miller, *Tropic of Capricorn*, on a tape just for us! We could never have afforded it, but hey, it never hurts to ask right? We didn't. We wished we had. After gigs, we would get the student volunteers whom we had requisitioned to help schlep our gear back to the van, to pass around a bottle of Wild Turkey 101, take a swig, and repeat the following words:

"This is not art. This is a gob of spit in the face of art, God, what you will!" and their initiation into the Henry 100 Club was complete!

Why the Henry 100 Club you ask? I'm getting there.

As we traversed the frozen wastes, listening to Balsam read Miller, and feeling akin to Miller's "inhuman ones," I fished out from our box of books *The Miller-Durrell Letters*, and like magic, opened to a life-changing missive from Miller to his new acolyte, Lawrence Durrell. Durrell was in his twenties and then residing in Corfu; Miller was in his forties, struggling to make ends meet and failing magnificently, in Paris. Durrell had come across a black-market copy of Miller's (banned) first book *Tropic of Cancer* and was so blown away by it that he started writing a book of his own imitating Miller's style. *The Black Book*, he called it. In the meantime, he wrote fan letters to the ex-patriot American and sent him samples of his own writing.

In these early letters to Miller, Lawrence Durrell lamented his frustration with the "racket" called publishing. Miller took an instant liking to the ex-patriot Englishman, and wrote back from the Villa Seurat, in Paris. It was the summer of 1936, but it could have just as easily been the winter of 1988, or today, for that matter, and his letter could have just as easily been addressed to two writing working musicians, slugging their way through the blizzards of bullshit that are the American recording and arts industry in general.

After some brief commiserations, Miller got down to business:

> Listen Durrell, don't despair yet. If you have the guts for it the thing to do is to go to the bitter end, in your writing I mean. If you can possibly hold out, and I imagine you can, write only what you please. There is nothing else to do, unless you want to become famous. They will shit on you anyway, so have your say first. I'm not recommending obscenity necessarily. Each man has his own way of being himself and of saying it so ultimately that he can't be denied. Compromise is futile and unsatisfactory.

As Hunter S. Thompson might say, here comes the wisdom, the kicker, the template and business plan on which I depended for the rest of my professional life.

> You will always have a hundred readers and, if they have taste and discernment, what more can you ask? Even when you elect to be absolutely honest it is difficult. Expression seems such a natural, God-given thing—and yet it's not either. It's a life-long struggle to find yourself. Think of Cezanne, Van Gogh, Gauguin, Lawrence. Think of Dostoevsky—or Titian, if you will. Think of the autobiographical documents: they teach you more than anything...

This piece of writing hit us both like a nourishing warm breeze. Soothing, reassuring, liberating. From that moment on, we catered to our tastes, and ours alone—in our songwriting and compositions, our approach to our audience, as well as business people, and in defining who we were and what we were about.

"You will always have a hundred readers, and if they have taste and discernment..." they can go out and get you another hundred we reasoned, and they can get you another two hundred, and on and on. There it was, the blessedness of networking. And weren't Miller and his friend Alfred Perlès doing just that? Clearly, they had gotten the young Durrell to sign up for subscriptions to their projects, like writers did in Balzac's day. The multiplication was working. And if it could work for them, it could work for us!

Over the course of their correspondence in these early years, Miller laid out his plan and the underpinning philosophy that would hold it all together. About a certain publisher's "plan" for Durrell's career, Miller was candid with his young pupil:

> With that attitude you'll always be fucked good and proper. Don't you see, according to *their* logic, you *must* conform—because they control the situation. But the moment you say to hell with that and decide to do as you damn please *you find the man to sponsor you.* Yes, as you say, our fancy weather cock may turn down your book—it will be Greek to him, that I can tell you in advance. But, canny bugger that he is, he may decide to publish and blow you to the skies, because few *others* have seen merit in your work. One never knows with such guys. But, anyway, whether he refuses or rejects, whether you lose out permanently with Faber or not, all that is beside the point—that is their affair. Yours is with your own conscience. On that grain

of faith on which you built your book you must rest. You stand firm and let the world come round... The only thing that truly nourishes is the doing what one wants to do. I tell you, everything else is crap, and futility, and waste. Let the angel be your watermark. If no publisher exists for you we will have to create one.

In a subsequent missive addressed to both Miller and Anaïs Nin, young Durrell says he's been attempting to write, more commercially, under the pseudonym Charles Norden:

He (Charles Norden) is the double I need—not for money or any of the fake reasons I'm always giving—but simply for a contact with the human world. I am so alone really that I am scared of going crazy; Norden will keep me in touch with the commonplace world which will never understand my personal struggle...You see, I CAN'T WRITE REAL BOOKS ALL THE TIME...what I want is this, frankly. Once every three years or more I shall try to compose for the full orchestra. The rest of the time I shall do essays, travel-books, perhaps one more novel under Charles Norden.

Miller shot right back:

Don't, my good Durrell, take the schizophrenic route! If there are just a half dozen people in the world, like myself, who believe in you, that should more than outweigh the other considerations. The danger is to the psyche—believe it or not! You are young, happily married, full of encouragement, praised to the skies, healthy, not hungry, not penniless, befriended, surrounded with congratulations, with what not, a boat to boot, be Jesus! the Ionian skies, isolation (which I would give my shirt to have!), and so on.

Here Miller is the kindly father figure. There's no way Durrell could possibly have known at the time that Miller had no shirt to give, was going days on end without food, had been begging on the street, sleeping on park benches, ashamed to show himself, as he says in *Cancer*, "without a button on my fly."

And this is where Miller's Taoism comes in. Taking life as it comes. Trusting that if one's heart is true, one's self fully formed and at peace with his or her consequences, that survival is the reward. That love happens. That whatever ensues, it happens because the real you made it so. That message is liberating, esteem generating, and ultimately empowering. My bandmate Alvis and I were the sole generators of our own bona fides. We wrote songs against conservatism such as "This Speech Is Free," "Talk About Me at Work Tomorrow," "Yuppie Drone," "Living in Exile," "The Galactic Funny Farm," "The Great Rondini" (about Reagan's chicanery), "Money Go Round," "It Ain't Easy Being Green" (a riff on the difficulty of being environmentally conscious), "Ecological Disaster," and the song that got us started, "Feminine Deodorant Spray Makes Me Sneeze." Those and dozens more played all over the world (and made us just enough money to live on, barely). We performed these in front of conservative audiences who sometimes walked out, but by and large were moved, appreciative, and sometimes left the venue with a new perspective, and maybe, a song in their hearts. We held our heads high and soldiered on.

Meanwhile, Henry also had some tough love for the young Durrell when he sensed Durrell's courage flagging, as we all have succumbed to weakness in the face of cruel adversity (and bad reviews) from time to time.

Now don't, my dear good Durrell, ask me to weep with you—because you are *alone!* You ought to be proud of that.

Hear! Hear! Says I!

If, as you say, you can't write REAL books all the time, then don't write. Don't write anything. I mean. Lie fallow. Hold it in. Let it accumulate. Let it explode inside you... A man can fall down, can undo himself, can go haywire—but he ought not to deliberately incarnate a lesser self, a ghost, a substitute.

And why couldn't you write all the other books you wish as L.D.? Why can't L.D. be the author of travel books, etc.? What's to hinder it? And it's wrong to think you are cutting yourself off. On the contrary, you are muscling in.

And here's one last bit, the part where Miller gives the young man the antidote to all the angst, worry, and insecurity this holy path he has just outlined may bring to the young writer's future.

Tao, me lad, and more and more of it. I'm wallowing in it. It's exactly my philosophy—every inch of it—even to the contradictions—precisely the contradictions. It's in my blood—and I am scouting about now to discover if I haven't really some Tibetan, some Mongolian blood somewhere in the line... No, everything is there in the Tao business. Clear as a bell, says I. If you see the truth you can't help but obey it. There are no two ways. It's always the straight and narrow path—and a damned jolly path it is, when you hit it full on.

After my musical career wound down, I took some time off to read and write and, in doing so, I gravitated toward small press publishing. The reason was simple. I no longer had the youthful luxury of submitting and waiting, then submitting and waiting. Also, as I got to know other writers, I would watch them plead and beg with agents and publishers to get their unknown selves out there (and if you don't already have a built-in audience to bring to the table, good luck, because selling is hard, and these people hate hard work. They want projects that sell themselves).

But time and again I've watched good writers take the advice of some buffoon that goes something like this: Great idea for your book, well written, but the trend these days is for an open-ended ending, or what people want these days is a little more mystery, or work on the mother/daughter thing more, or... you get the idea. Whenever I hear some fatuous know-it-all businessperson start telling me what people want, I close my ears and the door behind me on my way out. Because, and listen carefully, no one knows what people want, because people don't know what they want until they see it. So, the poor writer spends another year or two rewriting an entire draft only to find said agent has moved on, changed his or her mind, or determined that the trends are now trending away from your topic, or they've given up the trade all together, and in the process thrown the writer's delicate equilibrium completely off track. The book seldom gets finished, rarely, if ever, published, and you can't get the time they made you waste back.

So, as with most things, the difficult way is most always the best. Take Henry's advice; if you're any good, go find a hundred folks who like your work, enroll them in the Henry 100 Club, and set them in motion to go get you another hundred, and before long, you won't need anybody. That's what this social media thing is ultimately all about. But even here there's a catch, because the way capitalist structures operate, everything that succeeds gets co-opted sooner or later. The Internet and social media are no exception.

Henry is absolutely correct in advising one to "First, have your say." That's why you were writing, composing, acting, painting, and making art in the first place, right? Unless, of course, your true motivation is some ill-informed and delusional fantasy on how to get rich, or because you love the sound of your own voice, or have fallen in love with the mirror. If that's the case, neither Henry nor I can help you, and wouldn't want to.

Think about it, have your say, then rustle up a small army, and muscle your way in. Henry and I both will love you for it.

P.S. Durrell went on to write many travel books, great novels, and nearly everything else, under the name Lawrence Durrell. He and Miller were friends for life.

PART II

THE
WORLD
OF
YESTERDAY

Who's a Good Boy?

Almost any band, combo, or solo act would sound good on a deck overlooking the Occoquan River just south of the nation's capital, on a lovely summer Sunday afternoon. Good food, cold drinks, pretty people all enjoying the sublime pleasures of fine weather, and no worries.

So, when the young man named Gary strolled up to me during our break, while my musical partner was going from table to table signing up patrons to our newsletter mailing list, I said sure, you can buy me a beer. As we leaned against the railing sipping our beverages, watching the river flow, he asked casually what we charge for a bar performance. Thinking he was just making conversation, I quoted a price five times what we were making that afternoon.

We were taking any and all jobs offered back then, self-financing our next record, with a plan to shift out of low-paying bars into colleges and better venues in the fall, but we weren't there yet. And the bills had been piling up.

When the fellow didn't flinch at the price, my eyes lit up.

"Do you own a bar?"

"Sure do. We've only been open a few months and I think you guys would be perfect."

Music to any working musician's ear!

"So, tell me a little about your venue," I asked.

"Well, it's a bit of a hike, south of here, in Southern Maryland. I bought it last winter and I've just refitted the place with a good stage, new lights and sound. The place can hold two hundred people, and I can give you several weekends, say Thursday, Friday, and Saturdays. Between now and Labor Day, the calendar is pretty open."

I did the math. At the fee I had quoted him, I really didn't care where it was, or who frequented the place. All's I could see was the rent getting paid, the car fixed, maybe an extra player or two for the recording we wanted to do that fall.

We booked four weekends, three nights each.

Now, we called ourselves The Pheromones, the chemical that creatures give off that attracts or dis-attracts potential mating partners, and we had some clever songs to illustrate the point. I usually wore a seersucker sport coat with a pink flowery Hawaiian shirt, and a fat pink carnation (fake) in my lapel. My hair was crazy. Hey, musicians are expected to be different, are we not?

"It's called Mutts," Gary said. "You can't miss it," he said.

So, for our first night, we took separate vehicles, and I was an hour and a half out and still couldn't find it, traveling up and down the four-lane tree-lined thoroughfare, until I finally caved and pulled into the only structure on the route, a one-story, windowless, white-washed building with a guy sitting on the stoop drinking from a bottle in a brown paper bag.

"Mutts? Never heard of it. Unless it's the place around back."

Around back was a single mirrored glass door. A single door only one person could fit through at a time, hardly the entrance to a venue big enough to hold two hundred human beings, but maybe they never heard of fire codes in this part of Southern Maryland.

I grabbed my guitar and Anvil case from the back of the vehicle, took a deep breath, and approached the mirrored door, pulled it open, and stepped inside.

It took a minute for my eyes to adjust to the darkness.

Before I continue, I feel I must proceed under the caveat that I would not normally mention race in the depiction of an individual or a crowd of individuals. But I feel it important in this instance to mention that the place was indeed, large enough to hold two hundred folks, and that was approximately the size of the crowd awaiting us. Two hundred Black, male, factory workers, enjoying a little downtime after their shift. I'll confess openly, and without pretense, that there isn't one drop of what one might categorize as "soul" in either one of us, nor in any of our skinny white-guy songs. This was going to be interesting.

As I stood there, taking it all in; the stage, big and beautiful to my immediate right, a phalanx of small tables reaching all the way back to a very large oval-shaped bar, with two hundred pairs of eyes on me. I smiled. I waved. No one waved back.

I parked myself on a bar stool knowing that Alvis, my partner, was at this moment trolling up and down the highway outside, as I had. Perhaps, even at that very moment, he was speaking with the tatterdemalion out front sipping from a paper bag.

Is it perverse of me to admit that when I saw him, tall, dark, and fussy, step into the bar called Mutts, in his pink satin tour jacket, glittery pink tie, and matching pink Converse high tops, the look on his face as two hundred burly male factory workers looked him up and down disapprovingly, my brain took his picture and immediately filed it in my "For When You Need A Smile" file?

I'm enjoying it even now, even thirty-six years later, and feel the joy. Then, of course, the horror.

Our first song was the Beatles' "From Me to You," always a crowd pleaser, which we rendered with sparkling harmonies and a clever chord progression. As we sang and played, men from at least a dozen tables scattered throughout the venue got up, and began gathering their things.

Our second number was an original we called "The Galactic Funny Farm," about how the Earth is really an asylum for the lunatics from around the galaxy. It's an idea we plucked from a short story by Voltaire called "Memnon."

And another dozen tables prepared to get up and leave.

Remember that slender mirrored door? The one that made me wonder if the fire marshal would approve?

Well, those factory workers, unable to exit any other way than one at a time, politely formed a queue, and, one step at a time, began to exit the building.

We tried another original, "Talk About Me at Work Tomorrow," about the mind-destroying sametude of the everyday workplace.

And another dozen tables got up to leave the bar.

"Dixie Chicken."

And another dozen tables full of people got up to leave the bar.

Now, my partner Alvis was a veteran of the band-gigging bar scene. He had groomed me to replace an old partner. I was a writer, could play a little guitar. I was a good singer. We wrote songs together well. We even had a couple of records that were making their way around the country, too.

"Good Lovin'."

And another dozen tables got up to leave the bar.

By now the line to leave the building reached from the slender mirrored door all the way to the back of the bar, then around the back wall, and was coming in our direction all the way down the other wall.

And I started to laugh.

By ones and twos they came, from all around the room, to stand at the end of the line, which, any minute now, would reach the side of the stage where I was standing.

I started laughing harder. I was finding it hard to stop.

"C'mon Jim, pull up," Alvis said off-mic, and launched into one of his own numbers.

But the line at the door didn't stop. One step, open door, exit, one step, open door, exit, one step, open door, exit.

You've heard people say, perhaps, they were in hysterics?

But have you, ever, really, been in hysterics?

One step, open door, exit.

One step, open door, exit.

I was laughing so hard tears were rolling down my face.

One step, open door, exit.

One step, open door, exit.

I put my guitar down on the floor of the stage, not trusting myself to fit it into the guitar stand right behind me.

One step, open door, exit.

And the crowd at my end of the stage kept welling, like water backing up around a broken pump.

One step, open door, exit.

One step, open door, exit.

I sat down on the edge of the stage, my legs dangling, laughing and geezing. I was starting to drool.

One step, open door, exit.

I put my face in my hands, weeping and laughing at the same time, finding it hard to catch my breath.

One step, open door, exit.

Imagine your entire body slowly going into a full-body charlie horse, through laughter that becomes convulsive, spasmodic, eternal.

One step, open door, exit.

One step, open door, exit.

Alvis finished the song he was playing and said into the microphone, "Thank you very much ladies [there were none] and gentlemen, we're going to take a short break. But we'll be right back, and we've got three more sets to play for your enjoyment this evening."

Alvis and Gary scraped me off the stage still weeping, my arms over their shoulders, and helped me all the way back to the bar. I was slowly resuscitated with strong drink and French fries. We watched the bar empty out the rest of the way from there.

"Well Gary, I'm sorry, but I think it's pretty clear that we're not the right guys for your venue, so if you want out of our contract I will certainly understand," I said when I was at last able to speak.

Alvis's expression turned to one of alarm. I was sure he could see the big golden bag of money that had sweetened his dreams ever since that day on the deck over the Occoquan River sprouting wings and heading for an open window.

"It's okay, champ," I said to Gary, "these things happen all the time. Live and learn, eh?"

"No fuckin' way, Mr. Pheromone," Gary was becoming indignant. "I love the shit out of you guys, and I don't care if nobody comes, you can play just for me."

"But, Gary..."

"You guys draw a nice crowd wherever you go, and I'm sure if you play here long enough we can open this place up to a bigger audience, heck, people hear you on the radio!"

"No, no, Gary, you see..."

"No, you see, after you've played here a month or more, we'll grow the audience together."

Alvis was pleased.

I was fucked. Tears were coming back.

Eleven more nights.

We started bringing unfinished song ideas, the charts for songs we wanted to cover during our fall tour. We tried to hard-sell our audiences from town that this would be a really cool thing to do. A musical excursion. One night, about four tables of truly die-hard fans made the pilgrimage.

They left early.

Our wives took pity and made the trip.

They left early, too. But they had to form a queue, take one step, push open the door, and step outside.

HERMES AT THE SPOUTER INN

I was in the middle of a blissful summer, although I didn't know it at the time. I was between jobs, careers really, and more importantly, between girlfriends, or, if you prefer, women of interest, significant others, special lady persons. They say that a man's brain reaches its maturation point at twenty-seven years, and, at that very age I was really feeling it. Bad luck, personal catastrophes, and a paucity of viable options forced me to face the fact that if I wanted to be a writer I bloody well ought to create an environment for myself where I could do just that. So, I saddled up, and headed due north for an island called Clovelly, on a lake named Lovesick, in a country called Canada.

I arrived there spiritually hungry, heartsick, and starved for brain food. Gradually, my mind began to open what felt like huge empty vaults that needed filling. The more time I spent crawling back into my own skin, getting to know myself, the more I began to explore what I had been doing with my life up to that point. And what had I done? Well, I had learned the value of hard work, and that sometimes it doesn't get you anywhere. I also learned that I had great compassion and was capable of selfless love. I had walked away from two brutal car accidents and was nearly done in by a third. My heart had been broken, and then it healed. And, of course, was broken again.

I was not in need of new experiences. I had those aplenty. I had stood atop Pisa's leaning tower and looked down. I had stood in the chapel in Rome and looked up. I loved Wordsworth, and Eliot, Baudelaire, and Rimbaud, Alexander Pope, Keats, Steinbeck, Hesse, and Bob Dylan, yet I felt unschooled. What I needed was to be alone, to assimilate all that had happened to me. I needed to read deeply and to think more deeply. My secondhand car was now filled with secondhand clothes, a beat-up guitar, and boxes and boxes of books. I would return someday, I knew that, but I would not be the same man who had fled the scene. Fine, let's meet the new guy and give him a leg up.

So, I was in the second year of this hermitage when the phone rang. It could only be a relative, someone from the mainland, or one of the few hand-selected peeps who actually knew where I was. Usually, I could tell by the time of day who was calling. If I was reading, or writing, or just gazing at the universe, I would let it ring.

But a guy gets lonesome.

"Jimmy! I found you!" a woman's voice, full of relief and surprise, hit me in the ear. Damn if she didn't sound familiar.

"Hey there, so you have," I said, clueless as to who it was.

"Well it's a miracle! Strangely, all the information you gave me when you left town turned out to be wrong!"

"That's hard to believe," I plopped into a chair, praying for a clue. The late summer sun shimmered on the rippling waters outside. Birds were chattering. The breeze off the lake was divine.

"Well, forget about it, the good news is I found you, and do you know what month it is?"

"August?"

"That's right, and...?"

"And...the Perseid meteor showers are about to start any night now, should be dazzling if it's not too cloudy."

"And, Mister Forgetful, *we have a date!*"

That voice. Pleasant, playful. She knows she's fucking with me. But she means it. Yes. Green eyes. Long red hair. Petite. Earnest. Sprightly. Unrelentingly sprightly.

Suddenly I'm sitting at a trendy bar outside Washington, D.C. A year ago, late summer, early autumn.

That voice.

"I thought I'd find you here."

"Did ya now?"

"Remember? At Tommy's party the other night you said you loved baseball. You said you liked to pull in here for happy hour Tuesdays and scalp tickets. And voilà! It's Tuesday and I have two tickets to Baltimore-Boston up in Charm City tonight. *We have a date!*"

She was right. I had gone home for a month or more to see my folks, cash a few checks, maybe...catch...a...ballgame.

It all came flooding back. Triple sec, Rose's Sweetened Lime Juice, good vodka. Local bands, movies, a day trip to a battlefield, a picnic, her place, my place, somebody else's place. Her...name...is...

"JANE!" Jane Smedleton. "SMEDLY!"

"There you go! Now who's a good boy? You remember!"

"You know I'm in Canada."

"Of course, and you know I'm in Bethesda. And you also know that before you left, I told you that the third week in August I always visit my cousin and her husband in Nantucket for a week, and you agreed to meet me at Hyannis Port next Friday for the ferry to the island."

"But, Smedly, that was years ago."

"Wrong. It was just eleven months ago."

Right.

"But, you know, a guy forgets."

"Of course, I never expected you to remember. But when I found out where you were, I sent a letter to your local post office addressed to *Hold for Jim Patterson*. Pick it up, your directions and times are all there, I already have ferry tickets, three p.m. Friday next. Now look, I'll call again tomorrow. Bring a raincoat. As you always say, 'More later!'" and she hung up. I could hear her laughing as the phone hit the receiver.

Smedly. She's one of those you'd never see coming. It's like falling for the old trick where someone touches the top button for your shirt and when you look down, they knock your nose with a knuckle. And falling for it every freakin' time they do it.

I must admit, I like women who are a tad smarter than me. And in this case that meant smart enough to know when not to expect too much. Smedly had that crisp East Coast intelligence I've always admired, and a concomitant twinkle in her eye that wasn't accustomed to taking no for an answer.

Come to think of it, I hadn't had a twinkle in a while.

Of course, I had no intention of going to Nantucket. Smedly was great and all, but if someone else pulled the stunts she did, you'd never go for it. To be honest though, she and I got along well. She was a talker. Good sense of humor, a little sardonic. Smart. Her perspectives were surprising, mildly insightful, and aside from her low opinion of my personal life decisions, we agreed on almost everything else. She hung out on the periphery of my old gang of cheloveks (read *cronies*). Anyway, I knew Smedly dated around; that was fine, so did I. Plus, sooner or later I would head back up north and who knew when I'd return.

So, as I sat there, with her sprightliness still echoing and thrumming in the air all around, for the life of me, I couldn't think of one goddamn reason not to go to Nantucket. I had even read *Moby Dick*, and believe it or not, really liked it.

In those days I was driving a used custard-colored Oldsmobile Cutlass Supreme with a meringue-colored top. My peeps all called it the Boston Cream Cutlass. It was a sweet ride, lots of horses under the hood, big wide wheel base, rear-wheel drive, leather bench seats. After bombing around the country in that boat for a couple of years, I had only this to say about the American automobile industry: a beautiful and magnificent era ended the day they stopped making cars you could fuck in. But I digress.

As fate would have it, at the appointed hour, I found myself standing at the Hyannis Port docks with her letter in my hand, a raincoat over my shoulder, and a small duffle bag with a clean change of clothes, a couple of books, and a journal.

I looked around. No Smedly.

Hmm, thought I.

Had I ever stood her up? If so, then this is payback. But I had never stood anyone up, knowingly. I stood there wracking my brain when the ferry boat blew its horn, fucker was loud. Still no Smedly.

Just as I was imagining how I would spend the weekend, maybe up in Boston, or looking up old college pals in Worcester, damned if an airport taxi didn't pull up and out she got, beaming with satisfaction that, as usual, all her plans had played themselves out to a tee. Tight white capri-style jeans and strawberry heels to match her strawberry hair. A baby-blue sweater over a tank top with something gauzy tied around her middle. Giant bug-eyed sunglasses, her signature. She carried a purse and a small baby-blue suitcase. Lavender perfume.

I was cooked.

Smedly had a good job. I can't remember what it was, but I do know she was good at it and it paid well. I was living off quarterly dividend checks from an investment I had made when I cashed out of a brutal manual labor gig a few years earlier, plus real small monthly checks from projects I had worked on in between. A friend's couch or rec room here and there augmented my living situation; my folks weren't much help, but might throw me a fish if they saw bubbles in the water from where I went down. What I'm saying is, for the career-minded female I might have been a fun date, but I was in no sense of the word a "catch." I was pretty up front about it. Smedly would frisk me to make sure I brought date money before we went out. Not kidding.

I had also suffered a couple of dismal failures and unexpected tectonics in my love life over the last long stretch, so given my current state of affairs, "getting serious" wasn't really much of an option. I discouraged it both in public and in the mirror. So naturally, I didn't see it coming.

Ah, the sea. Or at least the fishy/salty splashing mist from the water in the sound spraying in my face on our way to the island. Smedly took the little flask she knew I carried in my jacket pocket and pulled on it like a sailor. She liked to make out in public too, I had forgotten about that.

Her cousin and family lived in a big gray house on a street tightly packed with big gray houses. Mr. Rogers—the kids' TV guy—lived three houses down. Everyone was on the lookout for him, but courteous enough not to acknowledge him except with twitters and smiles. There were daily reports of him at the market, or out for a walk, or leaving the nearby apothecary.

Smedly's cousin had prepared a sitting room with curtained glass doors and a fold-out couch as a guest room for us. It was sweet. Her family was sweet. They had a toddler—a curly-haired little girl—and she was sweet. There was a new baby, too. Sweet, sweet, sweet. Dinner was fun. It was the kind of pot-banging, fridge-slamming, kids-laughing, plate-clanging affair that you don't realize you miss if it's been out of your life for a while.

After dinner, the little girl, in her PJs and ready for bed, crawled up on my lap with a stack of books and I read them all to her while everyone had after-dinner wine. We giggled and laughed and spoofed on each story, with me changing little details in every other episode and her scolding happily, "That's not how it goes!"

The little girl was starting her second week of nursery school in the morning. The biological ramifications of that news meant nothing to me.

Poor fool.

The following day, Smedly and I did girlfriend-boyfriend stuff. We rode bikes, explored the island, held hands, had a candlelight dinner in the little town, and crept back into the house after midnight and made love on the floor.

The next morning everyone in the house, except me, woke up with the poops.

Good Christ, it was awful. That sweet house full of sweet people had turned into a gruesome infirmary overnight. A five thousand–square foot defecating chamber. Adult footsteps running in the rooms overhead. Kids screaming. Bathroom doors slamming, toilets continuously flushing, kids crying, and poor Smedly. The washing machine in the room next to ours was on continuously. I would have run some errands for them, but I couldn't drive dad's standard transmission.

So, I expressed my most heartfelt sympathies to one and all and went sightseeing.

First stop was the whaling museum. I didn't know that when Herman Melville wrote *Moby Dick*, the great author had never set foot on the island of Nantucket, from whence the whole saga begins. I also had never seen up close the harpoons the nineteenth-century whalers used. These were mounted up on the walls above reach, lengthy, with heavy-looking hooked iron spearheads. Worse still is the imaginative reality suggested by the rowboat they had there on display.

"So here you go," I could hear my ship's first mate giving orders, "you're going to get into this little boat with these guys, see, and here, take this harpoon," long, like the balancing pole a tightrope walker might use for tiptoeing between skyscraper rooftops! "Now, we're going to row you out into the roiling sea, right up alongside the biggest water monster in the world, big as any dinosaur, and you're going to poke it with this thing, got it? The beast has two feet of blubber under its hide, so poke 'm good. If all goes well, we'll be home in a year or two and you'll be goodly paid." I must have been muttering some version of that soliloquy because a pleasant older couple, clean, with library quiet in their voices, looked at me askance and scuttled timidly away.

There was a cute little bookstore down the street from the museum. One of those ma-and-pa places that used to be everywhere. A labyrinth of rooms with different classifications stenciled on note cards tacked above each doorway, all neatly arranged according to their customers' tastes. I found one of their many editions of *Moby Dick*, the one with illustrations by Rockwell Kent, and read snippets from the later chapters.

Who can show a pedigree like Leviathan? Ahab's harpoon had shed older blood than the Pharaoh's. Methuselah seems a schoolboy... I am horror-struck at this antemosaic, un-sourced existence of the unspeakable terrors of the whale, which, having been before all time, must needs exist after all humane ages are over...

Wild good stuff methinks!

The store was closing. How long had I been standing there? On my way out, I bought an astronomy magazine; maybe I could get some stargazing in some night if the weather was right. I also checked to see what Henry Miller titles they had. I'd recently had towering epiphanies reading his first two books, and was deep into his third, *Tropic of Capricorn*. I noticed they had a fresh new Grove Press paperback edition of it on their shelf, and that made me smile. I had the same edition in my back pocket.

My tummy was rumbling, it was time for dinner. The season was changing. The days were getting shorter. Northerners always go into a brief shell of mourning when they realize summer is about to abandon them, always too soon. And now the sky was a darkening gray that matched the gray shingled roofs and houses all around. And as lights blinked on here and there, as the air grew cold when the sun ceased to warm the moisture in the breezes, I looked around and there it was.

The Spouter Inn.

A painted wooden sign hung on links from a harpoon arm jutting from the wall above the door where a single lamp lit the way.

It was a cozy little pub turning over from afternoon to supper. Some woolly musicians were setting up on a small stage to the right, taking their time, peppering each other with jokes and jibes as they uncoiled cables and set up monitors.

The bartenders and wait staff were changing shifts. The place was filling up quickly and, after a brief stop in the loo, I phoned Smedly's cousin's house to check in. Everyone was puking and pooping simultaneously now. No need for me there.

There was only one spot left at the bar after I hung up. I took it, and ordered a rye and soda, no fruit.

On my right, the handsome older couple I had seen at the museum smiled wanly, made room, then turned their backs and didn't make eye contact with me the rest of the evening. On my left, was a guy about my age, elbows on the bar, forehead in his hands, dark hair spilling through his fingers, a glass of straight whiskey, neat, in front of him, staring intently down at a book he was halfway through, glued to the page. He was making low guttural sounds of surprise and astonishment.

That was oddly comforting.

"Have the fish sandwich," the bartender gave me on the QT. Okay. I sipped my drink and thumbed through my magazine.

When the fellow on my left's fish sandwich arrived, he closed his book, and looking around, noticed my magazine.

"You an astronomer? If you are, you've come to the right place. The skies here at night are dazzling. If the weather is right. There's an old lighthouse at the other end of the island, no longer used to warn ships, of course, but they've got a pretty good telescope up there, and on Sundays for two dollars you can climb up and have a look."

"No, not an astronomer by any stretch, but I do love stargazing and I like to keep up with any news of asteroids and comets heading this way," I smiled. "So, thanks for the tip. Sunday's my last night, so I'll definitely give it a whirl. So uh, what are you reading?"

"This!" he slapped his paperback down in front of me. The cover had a black-and-white photo of an elderly man in tweed smoking a pipe and flipping through a manuscript of some sort, most likely of the book itself resting before me. It had a broken spine, turned-down pages, ballpoint-ink marks where his hasty underlinings had skipped off the page. *Memories, Dreams, Reflections* by C.G. Jung.

Looking at that book, I felt we had somehow slipped out of or sidestepped time. I looked at the young man beside me. He had become Hermes, the trickster messenger god, delivering the goods, take it or leave it.

"You're like me," I chuckled. "I really use a book, I mean."

"Yeah? Well, this is the best book I've ever read. It's changed my life. The only book I ever finished reading and went right back to page one and read it through again. I'm looking through it now, can't seem to part with it. Do you know this guy?"

"Only tangentially, something to do with Freud, maybe? I have come across the name frequently, I'll say that."

"Well, this guy kicks Freud's ass! When they met, Freud was so amazed at this man's capacities for pure thinking that Freud passed out!"

"Like they had some kind of brain duel?"

"Exactly! And this is his way of looking back and sharing his secrets, how he invented whole new avenues of psychology, how he could figure out what drove people insane. When he was a little boy, the first dream he ever remembered was finding an old stone stairwell in the forest that led down to a long underground tunnel, and at the end of the tunnel was a giant cock standing straight up! His ability to reason led him to conclude that religion is bullshit."

"Kinda like this guy," and I slapped *Tropic of Capricorn* down in front of him. "I'm halfway in and it's already the best book I ever read."

And we were off to the races. He ranted and raved, in a good way, about the collective unconscious, archetypes.

"Jung had a pencil box when he was a schoolboy, and the box came with pencils and a ruler. Well, he carved a little figurine from the ruler. He even made a little woolen jacket for his new friend to wear. Jung had a stone he carried in his pocket, as little boys will, and he painted the stone half black, half white, and kept it in the pencil box with the little man and he hid them on a beam in an attic where he wasn't allowed to go. Think about it, man, no one in the whole world knew about his secret little man. And whenever he was down, or afraid, he would think about him, and know he was safe. Years later, he would wonder about his patients in the insane asylums and wonder where they had hidden their own little secret selves."

"I tried reading Freud's book on dreams but that kind of writing, the prose itself, I mean, makes me apoplectic," I frowned.

"Me too! Jung has written scores of textbooks, for scientists and such, but this is his closing statement, man, this is his summing it all up, his own self-psychoanalyses, plain, concise, to the point, nonclinical, he's after the humanity, and unlocking dreams, of others as well as his own, is a big part of that. So, for him, it's *the story untold* we have to discover and then get to the root of. It's about rolling up your sleeves and getting in there with compassion and honesty, but also with the do-or-die courage to face your very own worst enemy, your own unknown self, man!"

"Sounds like a dirty business," I laughed. By now the band had started and we adjourned to a drafty verandah where we could stay revved, drink whiskey, and chain-smoke cigs without having to shout over the music. "I think I'll follow your example with Jung and when I get to the end of *Capricorn,* I'll just turn it over and read it through again. His paragraphs are whole pages long and you get the feeling that his thoughts are about to run away with the writing, but there's story to it. You eat, sleep, drink, screw, and deal with whatever life throws at you, and it throws everything at you. He's honest about being a man preoccupied with getting laid. All his experiences are tossed into the telling of everyday conundrums; he's taking life as it comes with no overriding principle to guide him other than getting by well enough to write it all down. His plan is to have no plan at all. He's written a primer on the sanctity of desperation. Like your man Jung's memoir, it's the goddamnedest thing I ever read."

Eventually, my friend took his book and melted away. I wanted to make sure everyone was asleep when I went back to poopie palace, so I returned to the bar and caught the band's last set.

I took a long way back, strolling through Nantucket after midnight, back to the big gray house on the street of big gray houses. I smoked a couple of cigarettes on the back steps and ruminated on the course of my day and the passion of my Hermes-like Jungian stranger at the Spouter Inn. I thought about the frosty ghostlike couple from the museum, the band I had heard, harpoons, and listened to the quiet whispers of wind singing quietly all around me. I could taste the big wide ocean just beyond the rooftops. Then I crept back into the house. All was quiet, the atmosphere seemed clear, the dryer in the laundry room was rolling and tumbling, then it stopped. I crawled in next to Smedly and fell asleep.

I woke up late. The place was empty. Smedly left a note saying that everyone was feeling better and they had gone on errands. My tummy was rumbling in a strange and uncomfortable fashion. After a shower I stood in the bathroom brushing my teeth, I heard a noise behind me. A loud splat on the near wall. Fuck me if I wasn't power-blasting last night's fish sandwich uncontrollably all over everything! As I was cleaning it up, I barfed.

The proper anti-pooping medicines were by now at hand, but it was still another couple of days before I was anything approaching okay. I stayed in the bathroom. I slept in the tub.

Our last night there, feeling better, Smedly and I went down to the old lighthouse, paid four dollars, and climbed the stairs to the telescope. Seeing Saturn for the first time is an oh wow moment for even the most disinterested person, and as we went back outside, Smedly took me in her arms under the early autumn stars and kissed me in a way she never had before. Looking down into her eyes, there was something new there, too.

"I'm not going to say it first," she sighed in my arms.

I almost said, "Not going say what?" But it dawned on me what she meant. My heart sank.

I could but I just can't, I thought. As my eyes searched hers, I know I was looking at her like the Scarecrow looked down at Dorothy, with kind, sorrowful, eyes, on the Wizard's balloon platform, just before she left Oz.

Her shoulders sagged, she stepped back. The love light in her eyes dimmed. "You've done this before," she said. There was a knot in my throat I hadn't felt since I was a kid. If I had thought of something to say, I would not have been able to say it.

The next morning, before leaving Nantucket, I stopped into the little bookshop and purchased a copy of *Memories, Dreams, Reflections* by C.G. Jung. When I checked the shelf that held books by Henry Miller, I noticed their copy of *Capricorn* was gone.

Smedly and I took the ferry to the mainland, drank hot chocolate, and cuddled arm in arm as we watched the island slowly fade away. I gave her a ride to the airport. When we parted, she gave me a sad little smile and said quietly, "...but you know me..." and got on the plane.

When she was out of sight I nodded, yes, I do.

It was a long ride back to the Lovesick Lake.

The book was astonishing.

While Writing Roughnecks and Reading Moby Dick

According to Nathaniel Philbrick, author of *Why Read Moby Dick?*, Herman Melville had never been to Nantucket when he wrote his great novel. I find this reassuring. Yesterday I blew through the first forty-one pages of *Roughnecks* following Rose Solari's edits. Rewriting a sentence here, a word or two there, and as I go from the minutia of process to the complexities of character interaction—the myth, after all, being the sum and substance of the thing—fact will bow to fiction, and the myth I create regarding the meaning behind these concatenated episodes will begin to thread itself into a much bigger reality. Hopefully, one that will give a truer though slightly altered—for the better—form to the story I am telling.

I am reading *Moby Dick*, for possibly the sixth time, start to finish, while writing my own novel, *Roughnecks*. *Roughnecks* is a fictionalized account of my grade-school friend, Quinn O'Connell Jr.'s (AKA Zachary Harper), adventure in the American oil patch back in the late 1970s/early 1980s. We actually researched the book together shortly after the events themselves took place way back then, and, over the years, whenever I could carve several months out of my life to work on it I would. If I had been away from the project for a long time, it would take about six weeks for me to reboot my brain on the story and all its particulars before I could hope to add new material.

Reading Melville's sea adventure about hard-working men in a dangerous profession is just what I need. I reread *Moby Dick*, among many other inspiring works, in my six-week refresher course to help get me in the mood, to get back in stroke, so to speak. I then rework the manuscript from page one and by the time I reach blank pages, my fresh momentum hopefully will produce fresh new sentences. I have also stumbled upon some books and monographs on the whaling classic that have added clarity to my impressions of that work and help me to understand all the ways the book is dissimilar to my own. Suffice to say, I'm going for a simple form of osmosis to infuse my work with some good Melvillian joojoo, rather than an academic or deliberate approximation of tone, to influence my storytelling.

John Bryant, writing in *The Cambridge Companion to Herman Melville*, argues that

> Ahab is Democracy's worst nightmare; the charismatic, single-issue demagogue who can sway the masses away from mutual and communal contractarian democracy to self-destructive individualism or separation... Rather than have his characters spout politics in the subterranean recesses of being and sexuality, all the more to show us the human necessities of certain ideologies. Thus, readers experience in their reading why Ishmael chooses freedom and love; why Ahab demands control. Ahab himself describes it thusly, "It is not Ahab who is blind but our silent impersonal God, which cannot see that the mystery of being pre-exists divinity."

This "the mystery of being pre-exists divinity," caught my eye, because while soaking up books on Native American spirituality in the region where *Roughnecks* occurs, the Dakotas, northeastern Montana, and Saskatchewan, I learned that the term "Great Spirit" is actually a deliberate Christian misinterpretation. A correct translation of what has come to be called the Great Spirit would be "Great Mystery." This is important because it sidesteps the Judeo-Christian need to anthropomorphize, to make human, their vision of what God is, therefore subconsciously denying the alternative notion that what we're calling God is actually all around us.

Bryant continues,

> He (Ahab) has set up God as an unknowing, father figure version of himself, sans personality, sans self-righteous anger... We are Ishmaelian cosmopolites or Ahabian tyrants because our sexuality is conditioned by our need to fill a nothing through commonality or dominance.

Commonality or dominance. Socialism or capitalism? The herd or the individual? But more so, to my purpose here, it is how we approach the age-old conundrum of Being and Nothingness that determines which side of the iron wall of reality versus mysticism we choose to live on. That certainly is an underlying theme of *Roughnecks*, trying to peep through the tall grasses of the Montana hell-and-gone. Protagonist Zachary Harper is a combination of Ishmael and Sal Paradise (the narrator of Kerouac's *On the Road*) in that he remains detached, even while going through a near-total immersion in oil patch culture, and that slight detachment gives him cause to ponder, question, and accept his challenges. Like Voltaire's Candide, when he wakes up one day and realizes that he does not live in the best of all possible worlds. His response is to go questing, or as Louis L'Amour would put it, go "a-yondering." But will this "yondering" remake him into a Quixote or an Odysseus? Or will it just simply do him in?

Philbrick concludes his marvelous little monograph with a quote from *Moby Dick*, that Ishmael "doubts of everything earthly, and intuitions of some things heavenly: this combination makes neither believer nor infidel but makes a man who regards them both with equal eye." To which Philbrick concludes, "this redemptive mixture of skepticism and hope, this genial stoicism in the face of a short ridiculous and irrational life, is why I read *Moby Dick*."

A "redemptive mixture of skepticism and hope." A "genial stoicism in the face of a short ridiculous and irrational life." These make a good handrail, as editor Rose Solari would advise, to guide the reader through a narrative that takes us through a daily routine of lethal absurdities. It reminds me of a rather American form of mysticism, developed by the New England Transcendentalists and like-minded folk since then.

Once Philbrick and Bryant are done with me, I am free to move on to D.H. Lawrence and his treatment of Melville in *Studies in Classic American Literature*. D.H. Lawrence is a tricksy empath when he says,

> Poor Melville! He was determined paradise existed. So he was always in Purgatory. He was born for Purgatory. Some souls are Purgatorial by destiny... he really didn't want Eden. He wanted to fight like every American. To fight. But with weapons of the spirit, not the flesh...The mills of God were grinding inside him, and they needed something to grind on... they are grinding inside every American. Why? Heaven knows... Why pin ourselves down on a paradisal ideal? It is only ourselves that we torture.

Lawrence talks about what he calls "the Renegade," a person who would desirously metamorphose into a completely different creature from the one he was born. More primitive, more tribal. Lawrence wants no truck with the person who finds honor or authenticity in rejecting the forward push of humanity. I am comforted and simultaneously alarmed by his certitude in this, in part because my generation was in the ontological process of redefining what it is to be civilized. But somewhere in Lawrence's disquisition on Melville in *Studies in Classic American Literature* (a title that has always sounded tongue-in-cheek to me given the many lacerations found in this oddly funny little book), he questions Melville's ability to take life as it comes.

To take life as it comes.

It seems so simple.

Taking life as it comes has always been a natural thing for me, and I am always surprised that it is not so for most. "Wait and see," my father must have said a thousand times, each instance getting an eye roll from my mother who wouldn't have asked a question in the first place if she wasn't desirous of an answer. Like him, I think of options, and I wait and see. Zachary Harper too, stops, looks, and listens.

After having success with his Pacific adventure *Billy Budd*, Melville latched onto the true-life story of a ship called *The Essex*. *The Essex* had been rammed out of the water by an angry whale. Twenty or so crew survived. They were a thousand miles from the nearest known islands. But those islands were rumored to be inhabited by native peoples who were rumored to be cannibals. So the seamen decided to row three thousand miles instead, heading for South America and, of course, ended up eating one another as a consequence. White people. Jesus.

Lawrence's mindset is inherently progressive, refreshingly so. And therein lies his connection to generations, past and future, of what Henry Miller called his "inhumans," people who just instinctively reject the Judeo-Christian, the capitalist-puritan ethic which Lawrence disregards in an exasperated pique. "Good God, what does it matter? If life is a tragedy, or a farce, or a disaster, or anything else, what do I care? Let life be what it likes. Give me a drink, that's what I want just now."

A tribal member, a member of the herd, can hardly take life as it comes. The edicts, customs, traditions, and conditions of the tribe or herd dictate one's response to everything. That certainly is the trap even a Renegade can fall foul of. To be "Renegade," again, is anathema to Melville, according to Lawrence. It's one thing to be disillusioned, bankrupt; it's one thing to betray a trust, but to backslide, to regress? Unnatural. I guess we all draw lines somewhere. (And are we not special for it?)

But add to Lawrence's Renegades, and Miller's Inhumans, Melville's Desperados. "There is nothing like the perils of whaling to breed this free and easy sort of genial, desperado philosophy," Melville writes. Renegades, Inhumans, Desperados—Roughnecks. Now we're getting somewhere.

Both Philbrick and Lawrence make mention of Melville's personal disappointment with his inability to make male friends. Male interrelationships have been a theme of the *Roughnecks* project and one I have been keeping notes on for some time now. My take is that men are inherently suspicious of one another, and I'd like to leave it at that. But perhaps the very word has connotations that challenge the notion that a universal definition of friendship exists. Companion. Confidant. Acquaintance. Friend. Is it true that women seek community and men seek isolation?

A man, let's say, in lament over the dearth of male friendship in his life, ignores the choices he has made. To steer clear of confrontation and to have a strategy for when confrontation is inevitable. Is like-mindedness necessary for friendship to form? Is it even possible? Learning and deciding what and whom to trust must first require an ability to trust. The sacrifices, compromises, the risks taken, and more importantly, the risks avoided in his relationships with his fellow men, all reach a sum, add up to something. And when all is said and done, a man looks around to see if anyone is left still standing. There, he may at last find a friend...or himself, floating in open water, clinging to a wooden coffin.

Zachary Harper, in *Roughnecks*, will end up looking into a mirror and seeing a stranger look back at him, smiling.

Melville was writing his sea adventure about whaling when he was invited to spend a long weekend with a favorite author of his, Nathaniel Hawthorne. Did the women in their lives arrange it? The meeting is said to have meant more to Melville than Hawthorne, because when Melville returned home to finish his whaling adventure, there were a few significant additions to the plot. Namely a white whale, a crippled captain named Ahab, and a pagan harpooner! He dedicated his masterpiece to Hawthorne, and then a couple of years later, the two men had some kind of falling out. As I glide through what hopefully will become the final version of *Roughnecks*, I will hold to the notion I had at the outset, that the story should begin and end without contrivance. Like an average workday, like an average life. That there is enough drama, action, heartache, and controversy, enough tragedy and human interaction in the day to day of this story, to just let it all play out, as it will for all of us one way or another.

In *Roughnecks*, I felt that the oil underground, "the rich black blood of the sacred earth," was metaphor enough to evoke the native North American nature deities that permeate the history of this part of the world and help to infuse the narrative with a spiritual sense of connection between man and nature.

And I'll have my moments.

Chapter LXIX of *Moby Dick* is two pages long. It is called "The Funeral." In it, Melville describes the carcass of a whale being lowered into the ocean once the whalers have extracted from the dead animal all they can. He explains that the animal's corpse is so huge that once cast adrift, other mariners espying it from afar, observing breakers in the water around it, and ocean-going birds scavenging upon it, will mistake the beast for an uncharted atoll, reef, or shoal, a hazard to warn other ships to avoid for years to come. And Melville will have his moment:

> There's your law of precedents; there's your utility of traditions; there's the story of your obstinate survival of old beliefs never bottomed on the earth, and now not even hovering in the air! There's orthodoxy!

> Thus, while in life the great whale's body may have been a real terror to his foes, in his death his ghost becomes a powerless panic to a world.

> Are you a believer in ghosts, my friend?

Soon I'll be sorting through anecdotal information and hopefully the proper ones will announce themselves in the text. Perhaps even my own Hawthorne—Rose Solari—may steer my attention toward a summation, concordance, and integration of ideas as I march toward resolution. But those resolutions should be simply placed so that you find them only if you want to. In other words, no direct equivalencies.

But of the hundreds of interviews, out of a thousand anecdotes omitted for their redundancy, one was discarded because of its potential to overpower and commandeer the narrative. I was interviewing a Canadian man who had worked in the Williston Basin during the time I'm writing about. His stories basically affirmed the hundreds of others I had heard just like it. He told me nothing new, but it was good to get his affirmation that I was on the right track. As we were parting company, for some reason, I asked him what he had done for a living before he went roughneckin'.

"I worked in a giant slaughterhouse near Chicago. The cows would work their way down this zigzaggy maze until, one by one, they would step up to my station where I would fire a bolt into their brain. The floor would open up and as they fell through they would be gutted, blood drained, etc. I did that for a couple of years, and it really started to get to me. You know, when you think about the Nazis, and ask yourself, how could they have killed so many people, I think about that job. Let me tell you. After a while, I could easily see how you could replace those cows with people, especially if, like them cows, they didn't know what was about to hit 'm." That interview still gives me chills. Worse, any scene I put a story like that into would be overthrown, so I'm telling it here.

After Herman Melville died, and they were going through stacks of papers and dismantling the desk in the great writer's office, this quote from Schiller was found taped inside his writing desk.

"Keep true to the dreams of thy youth."

I have taken a blue Sharpie and written the same thing directly onto my desk just under where my keyboard normally rests. I realize that the older I get it is actually harder for me *not* to remain true to those dreams.

THE WORLD OF YESTERDAY

My father always said that his first memory was of standing on the couch in his parents' living room, small hands on the back cushion, peering out a picture widow at a neighborhood street in Bend, Oregon. There is a slow-moving line of cars and horse-drawn carriages inching its way down the lane. The line of cars is there every day, and every day he stands there and watches. His street is a long one, and at the end of it is the cemetery. He is not allowed to go outside to play. Death is all anyone talks about. Death from a great flu epidemic. Death from a great war just ending. Everyone has lost someone. Most have lost a few. It is 1918.

My parents were born during the First World War, my father in 1915, my mother in 1917. I didn't know my grandparents. I was raised on the other side of the continent. When I was in my teens and early twenties, the last of the WWI generation, then in their seventies and above, were all around me, and treated with quiet reverence by one and all. Armistice Day, November 11, was still celebrated with great fanfare. On the Lovesick Lake, where I spent my summers, most islands and cottages on the mainland were populated with people from the "between the wars" generation and their remaining elders from WWI.

In those years, our summer home on Clovelly Island must have been a comfortable place for the older ones to visit, as most of the look and feel of the place would have been very familiar to them. A big iron and wood barrel butter churn—now used for holding summer flowers—greeted them on the front porch. There was a fully functioning cast-iron wood stove in the kitchen that we depended upon for our meals, and smaller wood stoves in the bedrooms for heat. Coal oil lamps burned late into the evenings. There was a sawdust house for preserving ice, and an icebox, instead of a refrigerator, in a nook behind the kitchen away from the heat. A sundial on the front lawn kept good time. The benches and furniture, outside and in, were all handcrafted by local folk from local trees and timbers.

"You know, was a time, when everything in the world was handmade," laughed one old-timer when I pointed out a favorite rocking chair, constructed from a collection of hickory sticks and branches.

They called me a "history buff," because they needed an easy explanation for a boy who read all the time instead of hammering nails and tinkering with engines. But it would have been impossible to keep up with the adults around me if I didn't study up on their life and times. Every now and then, while sitting on the porch playing chess, or under a shady tree watching the world of the lake go by, one of these folks would open up about those days when they were young. Young like I was at the time. So, once in a while, during a quiet moment, the right question would open a door.

"I heard that you enlisted?"

"Oh, I enlisted because I hated my father," old Max Rishor told me on one of those afternoons.

"You hated your old man so much you volunteered to go fight in the worst war ever fought, thousands of miles from home?"

"Oh, Christ yes," he chuckled, "getting thousands of miles away from him was the reason to do it! He was a right old prick he was. A farmer, he must have beat me, all of us, within an inch of our lives, oh, I can't tell how many times."

"And you thought it safer to take your chances with the Germans?"

"Hell yes!" he laughed.

"And so...?"

"So, Father owned the only motor vehicle in the whole township. Had one of the first motorized tractors too. He taught me to drive so I could be a useful hand on his farm, which I hated. Anyway, as soon as I got the hang of this driving piece of business, I stole his car and ran away. I knew he'd kill me if he found me, so I drove to a recruitment center all the way down in Oshawa and signed up. I was only sixteen, but I was the only recruit who knew how to drive, so they took me anyway. Just before I shipped out, I sold the car."

Max looked like the cartoon character Mr. Magoo, with bald head, bulbous nose, and eyes in a perpetual squint, but that's as far as the resemblance went. There was nothing funny, doddering, or frivolous about the man. He was in his late seventies when I got to know him, and as real as ice on stone. He wore heavy black-rimmed glasses that were fashionable among serious people back then. His skin was like old leather with a few bristles of snow-white hair on his chest and over his ears. He shook when he talked, not for any medical reason, but because he got excited when he was telling a story. In the summer he always went without a shirt, so he was deeply tanned, and as with most men who live around the lakes, he liked to work outdoors all day. The most amazing thing about old Max was that mosquitos and deer flies wouldn't touch him. I'd be swatting at them every few seconds, the bites eventually outnumbering the kills, but not Max.

"The old fart still has that poison gas seeping from his pores, no doubt," my mother would quip when he was within earshot. He would grin devilishly, wink at me, and stick his tongue out at her when she turned her back. His tongue looked round and dry, like a parrot's.

He had been poisoned by mustard gas during the war. It burned his esophagus and stomach. The doctors had told him he could never drink alcohol again, so he drank his rye whiskey with whole milk. He could sip those all afternoon, and if I kept them coming, he might tell me a story.

"So, they looked the other way about your age because you could drive?"

He would begin every soliloquy by tilting his head back, squinting into a long-distant past, and say through a sigh, "Oh..." as his shoulders and hands shook, and ice tinkled in his glass.

"Oh... Christ yes, they needed people to drive the ambulance trucks from the front to the rear and back again. They didn't train me to march or crawl under barbed wires, nothin' like that. They said, 'You'll figure all that out as soon as you get there.' But they did let me loose with every kind of truck, car, or other vehicles they had. They didn't train me six weeks like the other fellas either, I was on a boat as soon as they could pack me off."

"You must have been wondering what you'd got yourself into though?"

"Oh, God! So, my first day over there I was driving this big truck toward the front and the shells just started dropping all around us! I yelled, 'What are they shootin' at me for?' You see, my truck had a great big red cross in a big white patch painted on the sides, you could see the son-of-a-bitch for miles! Like a big bullseye, a perfect target for the German gunners. They knew we were just going to patch those boys up and send them right back into the fight. So, I gathered some fellas around and we painted those red cross emblems green or brown to give ourselves a chance."

"So, you got to see some pretty gruesome shit your first day?" Max didn't mind the cursing, as long as we didn't do it around women.

"Oh," Max went quiet. I thought perhaps I may have gone a bit too far, maybe he was conjuring up scenes that were better left buried in his psyche, but no, he stopped talking because he saw my mother over my shoulder coming near. My mother brought sandwiches. He pointed to the chess board, "Your move," he said. We hadn't been playing.

When she moved off, he recommenced, sotto voce, his eyes open and penetrating, as an elder would when imparting a real-world secret to a younger male coming of age. "How those poor boys did scream and holler when we was haulin' 'em back behind the lines, beggin' me to stop, slow down, screamin' for Jesus, screamin' for their mothers. They had legs and arms half shot off, half torn to pieces with shrapnel, guts hanging out, bare bones sticking up, eyes and faces burned off. Half of them died on the way. We'd throw buckets of water on the floor to wash out the blood and guts for the next run if we had time.

"But the gas was the worst. There were different kinds of gas. Some gas would kill you pretty quick, not pleasant, but over in a hurry, I mean. But the mustard gas would sneak up on you, later sometimes. It lay for days, heavy, in the shell craters, trenches, and foxholes. Those poor fellas would jump in the bomb hole to get away from the shells without knowing it was there. You didn't even have to breathe it, it burned on contact. Burned their insides out slowly, drowning in their own blood, clawing at their eyes."

"So, it isn't true that shells never hit the same place twice?"

"Of course not, they hit the same spot over and over again, that's the bloody idea of it!"

"And you don't dare jump for cover?"

"You lie flat on the ground or curled up in a ball and hope one doesn't hit ya.

"So, after a few dozen missions I put in to be a driving instructor, so some other poor buggers could drive through the artillery fire and listen to them boys holler."

"But you were gassed too?"

"Oh, I'm not sure when, but we drove through clouds of it. Like fog. I probably got a little here, then a little there."

"Did the gas masks help?"

"They helped against chlorine, but the mustard stuff was different. Yeah, I was never without one though."

A WWI re-enactor I know reports that, even today, someone will purchase an authentic gas mask from the Great War and, putting it on, discover too late that the filter in the breathing mask was still caked with mustard gas. Now, a hundred years later, it will do its evil work.

Max's wife's name was Ella May. She was a good twenty years younger than he and still quite a looker. She was part French Canadian, had pale blue eyes and long dark hair, tied up in a bun. She used a razor blade to keep her eyebrows bare and penciled them in herself. She was good at it. She would vary the countenance ever so slightly from day to day with an upward angle or a downward turn. It doesn't work on most faces, but hers was perfect for it. Her long black hair only got lovelier as it slowly streaked with gray.

I'll wager that in the 1940s and '50s she was right in style, exotic, and turned every head. Ella May was great pals with my mother, Dorothy Rose, and that's how I knew Max. Max and I didn't have much in common. I couldn't tear down an engine, and was pretty useless in a tool shed, but I did bring cases of Metamucil—a concoction older folks use to keep regular—for old Max whenever I came to town, and flowers and butter tarts for Ella May. So, I was always welcome. It was Ella May and my mother who formed a local ladies' cocktail group. I was pouring drinks for them one afternoon when I overheard Ella May say that, "Old Max would get mad if you ever mentioned his dad, that is, of course, until Jimmy Patterson asked him why he'd rather face the whole German army than stay home."

Another WWI veteran lived across the lake. They called him "Feather," which was short for Featherstonehaugh. He had been stricken by gas too, though I can't remember which kind. Unlike Max, he had been torn up by shrapnel as well. His reconstructed stomach and abdomen bulged out like he had a bowl under his shirt. "A hernia," his wife explained. He would swim with a shirt on, but I would see him when he changed out of his bathing trunks. His lower abdomen looked like he had swallowed a bowling ball, and there were deep red gouges in his skin all over his torso front and back. There were also several small pieces of metal bomb fragments in his lower body that the doctors had decided to leave in. Feather drank his rye with milk too. To Feather, the origins of the Great War were not in any way ambiguous.

"Europe back then was ruled by royalties, kings and queens. All the royalties were related to one another. There was no such thing as Germany. They were Prussians. But in the 1800s, the French invaded Prussia, and the Prussians had to unify to fight back, and they did. That created Germany. To get even, they took a couple of French provinces as payback. Queen Victoria's grandson was the Prussian emperor, and he was the cousin of the czar in Russia. Well, the queen's grandson was a big fat dummy, and he wanted a war so he could be a big shot like his relatives in England and Russia. The great thing about America and Canada is we don't allow that kind of nonsense."

Although I saw Max and Feather together often at the same gatherings, I never heard them speak openly at the same time about the war because women and children were always nearby.

Ask Max about how the war started, he'd shrug and say, "Who cares? It's too late now."

Feather was an engineer and after the war he had gone on to become the president of an aircraft manufacturing company. Max had much more colorful postwar adventures.

Max and a few associates began building slot machines. These were illegal, but that didn't stop Max and his boys from putting them on a barge and taking them across Lake Michigan in the middle of the night to Chicago and setting them up in bars and speakeasies. One night, as they were making their way across the lake, they got the signal from shore to turn back. Each of the establishments that had a machine of his had been blown up by a "hot shot named Al Capone."

Decades later, they set up the same system for pinball machines. Max made a lot of money on these endeavors, but eventually he settled down and became a blue-collar efficiency expert. I imagine he was a pretty tough task master. They said he made a killing.

My parents had separated for a couple of years during the time I got to know Max. Mom had wanted Dad to retire before he was ready, and she returned to her native Canada and waited for him to come to his senses. But the big old house she lived in there could get lonely. So, Max and Ella May would have her over for drinks of a Friday afternoon, and usually she would camp out with them all weekend, cooking meals and playing cards or watching movies.

I would visit when I could, and dropping in on these three for happy hour cocktails or a Sunday brunch was always a fun time of boozy hilarity and great conversation. Also, if you have older people in your life, you check up on them often, just because. One Sunday morning I popped in after a trip to town where I had picked up some supplies they needed, but when I rang the bell no one came to the door. People didn't lock their doors back then, so I poked my head in and gave a holler.

"Anybody home?"

They were usually early risers, so I was mildly alarmed to hear everything so quiet. I set down the groceries and took a look around. Last night's empty cocktail glasses were on the coffee table. The ashtrays were full. Snack plates were here and there, and a trail of popcorn led back to the kitchen. I called out again.

"Is that Jimmy?" I heard Ella May mutter from the upstairs hallway. As I cautiously ascended the stairs, there they were in the hallway, all three of them, under a quilted comforter with lots of pillows, and I could hear them giggling from under the covers like school kids having a sleepover. The night before, old Max was in his cups and they had been helping him up the stairs when he just decided to lie down and go to sleep on the carpet in the hallway. Not knowing what else to do, they got some blankets and pillows and bedded down with him right where he lay.

"I, um, I'll just go down and get the coffee started, and don't worry, I can let myself out." I could still hear them laughing as I closed the back door behind me.

After all he had lived through, Max would have no truck with religion or the notion of God. On another Sunday morning, I popped in just as Dorothy and Ella May were leaving for church.

"Where are you two hussies going all dressed up, to a party on Sunday morning?" Max teased.

"To church, you old heathen, and if you had any concern for your mortal soul you'd change clothes and come with us," my mother scolded.

He gave a wry smile and said back, but winking at me as he said it, "It's your time, and your money, waste it however you will." But once they were gone, his smile faded. "What does God matter? You live and you die and you do what you have to do, God or no God. So who cares?"

And yet, on another Sunday morning, after I had spent the night in nearby Peterborough, the young lady whose guest I had been the night before insisted I attend church services with her after breakfast. There in the vestibule of the old Anglican Church was a giant bronze plaque listing the church donors of yesteryear to whom we should all be eternally grateful. At least a hundred names were immortalized in bronze, and there at the top of the list, his name bigger than all the rest, the number one church patron of all time, was none other than MAX RISHOR.

W hen the centennial of the outbreak of WWI rolled around, in 2014, long after Max, Feather, Ella May, and my dear

Dorothy Rose had departed the scene, there were several marvelous books published to commemorate the outbreak of the war. My favorites were *The World of Yesterday* by Stefan Zweig, *1913: The Year Before the Storm*, by Florian Illies, and *The War That Ended Peace: How Europe Abandoned Peace for the First World War* by Margaret MacMillan.

The World of Yesterday is a love letter to the world that was destroyed by both world wars. Vienna, pre-1914, with its high culture—opera, symphony, philosophy, nascent psychology, and literature—was Stefan Zweig's milieu. Before the Great War, eighty percent of those living in Austria-Hungary could read and write. Zweig admits that politics didn't concern him. He reports that he and his peers never voted. A friend to Sigmund Freud and Arthur Schnitzler, he once wrote to Freud, "Psychology is the great business of my life."

Zweig, a Jew, would go on to be the most translated author in history. Those are his books you see burning in some of the old newsreels of Hitler's Germany. He wrote his love letter to the past from exile in South America—exiled for the crime of being Jewish—and after he mailed his manuscript to his publisher, he and his wife committed suicide. That was in 1942. Hitler was in Paris. They must have believed he was there to stay.

The World of Yesterday is a deeply moving tract on freedom and culture, on intellectualism and its naïveté in dealing with the anti-intellectual barbarian mind. The pages drip with charm and wounded honesty. His depiction of sexuality, nineteenth-century style, resonates, as my parents' and grandparents' worlds were made of these mores that bent, broke, and were passed down, mangled and strange, to us born in the 1950s and 1960s.

"My literary work in the language in which I wrote it has been burnt to ashes in the country in which my books made millions of readers their friends." Zweig writes about the hideous desecration of the mind and body of culture brought about by the Nazis and the First World War which preceded them. "Against my will, I have witnessed the most terrible defeat of Reason and the most savage triumph of brutality in the chronicles of time."

1913: The Year Before the Storm, by Florian Illies, also takes a look, a last fleeting look, at what was left behind. The book is simply laid out in twelve chapters, one for each month of the year. It begins a few seconds after midnight in New Orleans, where a twelve-year-old boy is picked up by the cops for firing a revolver to ring in the new year. The next day he is sent to a detention center, the Colored Waifs Home for Boys, where the youth is so unruly, that, at a loss as to what else to do, the director hands the lad a trumpet. The youth was Louis Armstrong.

The book is a series of short vignettes, usually two or more to a page. Here, a young Joseph Stalin and a young Adolf Hitler go for a stroll in the same Viennese park every afternoon, but never meet. There, Franz Kafka goes to a movie theater and weeps.

We tour the art stalls in the baroque city of Dresden, then contrast them with the raw urbanity of the art being made in Berlin.

Meanwhile in Paris, Harry Kessler sleeps late, goes for drinks at the Ritz where he meets André Gide and Igor Stravinsky. Later that evening, tempers flare at a rehearsal of a new ballet by Nijinsky and Diaghilev, music by Stravinsky. Debussy is with them. Nijinsky shouts, and Debussy shouts, and Diaghilev shouts. They all repair to a bar next door and drown their argument in good champagne. All agree that the ballet will cause a great scandal. *The Rite of Spring* will indeed send shock waves through the art world from Moscow to New York. Coco Chanel and Marcel Duchamp are in the audience.

In 1913, intellectuals everywhere agree that a Great War is not possible because of globalization and the interdependence of financial markets. They say banks won't pay for it and industry won't support it.

In 1913, it's been a hundred years since the age of Napoleon ended and The Hague is planning a Peace Conference—for 1915—which intends to solve all as-yet-unresolved problems between nations.

One hundred and one years later, in March 2014, I attended a lecture by the Canadian historian Margaret MacMillan in Oxford, England. Her appearance was at Christ Church, in an ornate lecture hall which has been re-named the Harry Potter Room for the many scenes shot there for the movie series that bears his name. MacMillan is tall, slender, elegant, mature, soft-spoken.

"Since the Great War ended there have been twenty-two thousand books published explaining its origins," she begins, and then quips, "So here, for the first time, I can reveal the true culprits; it was the Canadians."

The premise of her book, and why it stands out, is an investigation of why Europe gave up on peace. After all, since Napoleon exited the scene a hundred years earlier, there had been a few minor dust-ups—including France's ill-fated incursion into Prussia—but nothing to rival the conflagrations that had raked across Europe in the previous centuries since the Reformation. In that century of peace, unprecedented advances in technology, medicine, education, transportation, philosophy, and the arts had gone unchecked, and culture went steamrolling into the twentieth century on a cloud of optimism and assuredness. A majority really did believe they were on the verge of outlawing war once and for all, eventually calling WWI the War to End All Wars. Societies for peace were cropping up all across Europe. Labor was getting behind disarmament and openly challenging conscription. Long chapters with titles like "What Were They Thinking?" and "Dreaming of Peace" introduce us to noble characters, now practically forgotten, who should have been household names—heroes and saints who turned the world away from wholesale slaughter.

Two characters really caught my imagination, and I instantly felt a kinship with each that was accompanied by a concomitant sense of tragic loss. It was as though I had stumbled across the fountainhead of ideas and ideals that had somehow been, vicariously, handed down to me from a previously unknown source. The first was Bertha von Suttner. It was she who cajoled and shamed Alfred Nobel, the arms and munitions manufacturer, into awarding a peace prize. Her international bestseller *Lay Down Your Weapons* hasn't been available in English for a long time. If it's possible to fall in love with a person who died a hundred years ago, I fell for her.

The other character to emerge from MacMillan's marvelous history is Jean Jaurès, a labor organizer, social activist, and peace advocate. Both of these people inspired millions. Jaurès was on an international campaign to get labor to refuse the call if conscription came. Days before the war broke out, Jaurès was assassinated in a Paris café, the very evening of the day he had declared to the authorities that he intended to continue to advocate for peace, war or no war. A plaque still marks the spot where he died in the Café du Croissant in the Rue de Montmartre.

Von Suttner died in bed a week before the archduke's assassination. She was seventy, and to my knowledge, no one suggested foul play. (There are no current biographies of either Suttner or Jaurès; you young biographers who love feminism and are anti-war, you know what to do. Get to work!) Archduke Ferdinand was, MacMillan tells us, the last statesman, or person in power, who might have stopped the war. He knew that should war come, the empire he was about to inherit, Austria-Hungary, would cease to be. Rasputin was stabbed in the belly the day the archduke was killed. The list of people who could have helped prevent the war who were murdered, killed, or died mysteriously in the run-up to Sarajevo is chilling.

MacMillan concludes,

> Liberals and the left as well as the peace movement attacked the arms race and its "merchants of death" at the time, and after the Great War, it was singled out as one of the main factors, perhaps indeed the key one, in bringing about the catastrophe. It was a view that had a particular resonance in the 1920s and 1930s in the United States, where disillusionment about American participation in the war had grown. In 1934 Senator Gerald Nye of North Dakota chaired a special Senate committee to investigate the role of arms manufacturers in creating the Great War and promised to show "that war and the preparation for war is not a matter of national honor and national defense, but a matter of profit for the few," ...what the arms race did do was raise the level of tensions in Europe and put pressure on decision-makers to pull the trigger before the enemy did.

Otto von Bismarck said, "Preemptive war is like committing suicide out of fear of death," and yet such reasoning, horrifically, is still seriously discussed today as a viable solution for our contemporary international disputes.

In her lecture as well as her book, MacMillan challenges some widely held notions. One, that the victors in war write the histories. Yes, the Treaty of Versailles at the end of WWI put crippling reparations on the Germans. The Germans, however, only made one partial payment of the first of three massive payments due. The notion that the treaty was the cause of WWII was Hitler's idea. Plus, the return to France of the confiscated provinces Alsace and Lorraine only seemed fair. No, she argues, it was the Great Depression that brought Hitler to power, igniting WWII. Nevertheless, by November 11, 1918, the day we now commemorate as Veterans Day, sixty-five million men had fought in the Great War, and there were forty million casualties—nearly ten million of those civilians.

As for me, I never have and never will accept the old adage that war will always be with us, or that the poor will always be poor. I do believe that several times throughout history humans have nearly succeeded in eradicating poverty and war. And I also believe we will never stop trying. In the meantime, books like these, and the memories shared by the likes of Max Rishor, Featherstonehaugh, Stefan Zweig, Florian Illies, Margaret MacMillan, and countless others, should make us all aware that war and poverty are not preordained.

Those who came through the Great War, the Great Depression, the Great Flu, and WWII experienced a daunting quartet of experiential training in tragedy, destruction, grief, and loss that marked those still standing as survivors, and they were either wounded, or cynical, or existential, or just bloody glad, and not a little astonished, to still be alive.

Many artists and intellectuals, and those savvy enough to smell trouble, fled Europe before all hell broke loose, twice. A century later, in 2011, my wife and I were touring the Modern Art Museum, Punta della Dogana in the Palazzo Grassi, Venice, where an exhibit was on display called "The World Belongs to You." Suddenly, the tragic genius of early twentieth-century modern art, a genre I had struggled at times to get my head around, suddenly hit me like a ton of bricks. When we entered one of the main exhibits, a room that appeared to be filled with junk shop relics, I was struck first and foremost with a smell that got my attention. It was burlap and earth. I recognized that smell vividly from a trip I took with others, when I was a teenager, to the Verdun battlefield in northwestern France. Burlap. Sandbags. Surveying the room, I saw nothing of the kind until I looked up and the entire ceiling was covered wall to wall with sandbags. And the meaning clicked. I had to sit down. I almost wept. Imagine your world completely destroyed by war. Most everyone dead. Well, when it was over, would you not consider the rubble that was left to be the holy relics of all your yesterdays? There was Duchamp's urinal with "R. Mutt, 1917" written on it. Another display was a room recreated from that era. A rocking chair with a broken doll, its forehead bashed in. Happy-go-lucky music from the 1910s played over and over on a scratchy ancient gramophone. The torso of a horse jutting out from a living room wall, as though the horse's head and front legs would be coming out the other side. A room filled with dangling light bulbs with a video of a dog running through a field. The horror of WWI is all over the art of the succeeding era and is best depicted through abstraction and surrealism.

Another room was an exhibit from 1943 called "The Roxy." You peer into a large room through a window. Dim lights, square and rectangular Persian carpets cover the entire floor. A jukebox plays happy songs from the 1940s. A portrait of General MacArthur is on the wall. The room is inhabited by mannequins. Mostly women. It is a whorehouse. The women are mutilated, cut in half. One has a rose sticking out of her throat, another a squashed face. The madam, facing the entrance, has a goat's head. Another room has nine marble figures, corpses lying under sheets. In another room there are three terrifying men with metal bodies. They are called *The Efficiency Men*. Suddenly you feel that entrenched elites of the late nineteenth century brought about the dual holocausts of the twentieth to forestall, eliminate, and destroy those fin-de-siècle ideas those same elites branded as degenerate—namely, world peace, socialism, women's suffrage, living wages, health care, science, tolerance of homosexuals, and the biggest threat to the old order of all, secular humanism.

Alfred von Schlieffen, the German general who concocted the prewar plan that once troops deploy there would be no calling them back, was from the German Junker class of war industrialists. He believed the threat of prolonged peace would eventually render his way of life obsolete. That threat still exists, and someday it will succeed; we are closer than you might think.

President Eisenhower changed the name of our national holiday called Armistice Day to Veterans Day to honor all American veterans. I still prefer Armistice Day. Honoring our veterans is, of course, a necessary and proper thing to do; we call it Memorial Day. Celebrating the end of war, or armistice, the laying down of weapons, however, is a different thing, and leaves open the possibility that we may someday celebrate the end of war altogether. Of course, it took a president/general to change the holiday from one celebrating armistice to yet another celebrating the military.

So it is that, during those rare intervals when there's a cessation of hostilities, armaments manufacture, and warfare, that civilizing forces begin to reclaim the field. Let's call it *Cessation Theory*. When the arts and sciences resume their inexorable progress. When humanism slowly, rationally, once again pushes back against the forces of superstition with guiding ideals. Education flourishes, and peace breeds prosperity. Before long, the universe of arms becomes threatened, and the wicked priests are deployed to legitimize the return of hostilities. We can look back through that historic lens and see that Napoleon ended the Enlightenment, Kaiser Wilhelm ended the fin-de-siècle, Hitler ended the avant-garde, Reagan ended the peace movement.

Maybe next time, a sufficient number of us will see it coming and break the cycle. It need only happen once.

Or we can keep making art from our broken and shattered lives.

Think about it.

STIRRING THE POT ON HENRY MILLER

JAMES M. DECKER AND NEXUS: THE INTERNATIONAL HENRY MILLER JOURNAL – A REVIEW

"Once you have given up the ghost, everything falls into place with dead certainty, even in the midst of chaos," opens Henry Miller's third book, *The Tropic of Capricorn* (1939). Anyone who has ever really hit bottom, and survived, knows the truth and wisdom packed into that sentence. From such a place there can no longer be any fear: fear of being misunderstood, fear of rejection, reprisal, censorship, failure, or even death.

Although he never regretted it, surviving in Paris during the Great Depression of the 1930s had proven a lot more harrowing than even the stalwart Brooklyn boy had predicted it to be. Sometimes homeless, always hungry, weeping on park benches, clutching his empty belly, which often went three, four, or even five days without a morsel of food, he was a desperate man, as he might say, "in every sense of the word."

And when at last he hit rock bottom, when his belly was screaming and he had bummed his last dime—clarity.

Having crossed that threshold—or given up the ghost—Miller was then free to abandon all pretense and, as he saw it, determined to write "all that is not contained in books." He wrote plainly and graphically about sex, he walked the labyrinths of love, philosophy, and art, telling the world, "I had no more need of God than he had of me, and if there were one, I often told myself, I would meet him calmly and spit in his face."

That kind of talk, throughout what Puritans still refer to as Christendom, could get you banned, ostracized, persecuted, and—ultimately and worst of all—overlooked.

> I am thinking that in the age to come I shall not be overlooked. Then my history will become important and the scar which I leave upon the face of the world will have significance. I can not forget that I am making history... (Henry Miller, *Black Spring*)

Once Miller found that voice, there was no stopping him, and his outpouring of words continued in a cataract of productivity that lasted until the day he died.

Books penned by Henry Miller as far back as the 1930s were banned in the United States, England, and elsewhere, ostensibly for the graphic sex in some, but also because of what the Citizens for Decent Literature called, "being opposed to the basic Judeo-Christian morality of the nation." Miller wrote thirty-two books, including literary criticism, novels, many books of essays, memoirs, travelogues, collected letters, and even a play. He influenced the Beats, the surrealists, and all the avant-garde who came after, and singlehandedly created the genre we now call creative nonfiction. Although the graphic sex for which he was condemned appeared in only a handful of his works, in many instances, all that was needed to evoke the censor's ire was the name Henry Miller on the cover.

The sixty-two court cases leading to the U.S. Supreme Court decision that eventually freed his works for publication also gave us the freedom we have today to write as we please. (The more famous cases against D.H. Lawrence's *Lady Chatterley's Lover* and James Joyce's *Ulysses* only pertained to those individual works. The Miller case ruling was all-inclusive.) Miller was an old man, in his seventies, when the ban on his work was lifted. Because of that Miller was virtually penniless for most of his life, even though millions had read and loved his work.

Miller is gone now. He passed in 1980 at the age of eighty-eight. At the time of his death he was famous the world over for very right and very wrong reasons. And as memories are short, and the issue of censorship resolved—for the time being at least—the controversies in which he was embroiled have faded.

And since then, post–sexual revolution gender politics, and an upsurge in conservative religious orthodoxy, has set his legacy adrift before it could be truly cemented. Hence, the window he opened on the world exists in a room whose door got locked, its key misplaced, and his vast body of work, with its myriad of intricacy, argument, and happenstance, remains unclaimed, unexamined, and in real danger of realizing his greatest fear, that of being *overlooked*.

Readers, artists, and lovers of the arts, particularly of the written word, have stood up many times over the millennia to resuscitate the works of worthy authors and artists.

It is said that T.S. Eliot resuscitated the works of John Donne; that without Poggio Bracciolini digging around in the basement of a German monastery in the early fifteenth century where he found the rotting pages of a poem by a first-century poet named Lucretius, we would not have had the prescient *On the Nature of Things*; that without Thomas Johnson reinstating the original punctuation to Emily Dickinson's poems in the 1950s, a century after they were written, the revolution of form and content in poetry she started would not have taken place. It took Alice Walker to rediscover the work of Zora Neale Hurston of the Harlem Renaissance, and Felix Mendelssohn painstakingly restored the music of Johann Sebastian Bach. August Derleth kept the work of H.P. Lovecraft alive until the right audience came along to appreciate it. Think of all that could have been lost. Think of all that has been lost.

Now enter a humble, soft-spoken PhD from, of all places, Illinois Central College, the indispensable home to thirteen thousand students from the Midwestern United States.

James M. Decker is a tall, quiet man who looks like he could be the great-grandson of Ray Bolger or Woody Guthrie. He moves about his classroom handing out reading assignments, pausing to answer a question, pointing out the tips of literary icebergs to students with big hair, wearing sports jerseys, loud T-shirts, and sagging blue jeans, a look I would call "post-cool."

No matter. His quiet, serious approach to educating has an unmistakably sincere feel to it, and that sincerity is what drives students, many of whom don't even take his classes, to seek him out during off hours in The Studio, ICC's writing center, in the English Department for guidance and help with thesis projects, form and structure issues, or simply in navigating the tricky labyrinths of higher education.

In other words, he is an unlikely and unassuming champion.

None of his students and very few of his peers even know that James M. Decker is the co-founder, publisher, and editor of *Nexus: The International Henry Miller Journal*, now in its fourteenth volume. And suddenly, Henry Miller's "age to come" has finally arrived.

"They are writing a void around him," Decker insists, "which is ridiculous when you look at who cites Miller as a major influence." So Decker did what so many courageous supporters of the arts have done before him—he took matters into his own hands.

Decker had been knocking around the idea of a Henry Miller journal as far back as graduate school, but it wasn't until he attended a Lawrence Durrell conference in Ottawa, Canada, in 2002, that the idea at last took root. It was there at a gathering of Miller enthusiasts, most notably Miller bibliographer Roger Jackson, Miller biographer Karl Orend, and others, that the subject of doing a journal on Miller was revived. "I'm not sure if Roger broached the subject or I did, but he was very enthusiastic. He would handle the layout and look of it, and I would handle finding people to write for it and edit it." Jackson started contacting other Miller collectors, and Decker set about "showing the scholarly community that it's okay to write about Miller, that there's a place you can send your article to. That we're all ears on all things Miller." Several Miller enthusiasts kicked in five hundred dollars each, and in 2004, *Nexus: The International Henry Miller Journal* was born.

(And so it came to pass, that in the summer of 2011, while reading the *Nexus* series, and gobsmacked by all it contained, I got in my car and drove from my home in Maryland, to Peoria, Illinois, and knocked on James M. Decker's door. We interviewed for three days. I attended one of his classes.)

MILLER AND THE CRITICS

As an educator, Decker knows that "the number one place where reputations are made is in the literary anthologies. Students come back to me time and again and tell me that something they read for me by an Edith Wharton, or a Jack

London, years later inspired them to read a writer's entire catalogue. That's how writers are passed along. Miller is not in the *Norton Anthology of American Literature*. Books are coming out even today about the modern American novel or the contemporary American novel, and Miller isn't mentioned at all, yet the writers he influenced—Pynchon, Mailer, Kerouac, Ginsberg, to name a few—are all there." Why?

Poet, playwright, novelist, and educator Rose Solari offers this analysis. "The scholarly mind looks for pattern recognition, that's why the unique individual doesn't fit well in the system of scholarship. We are hard-wired to look for and accept repetition, it is deeply ingrained; the first person who breaks a pattern goes unnoticed until a new pattern forms and their work is widely imitated." Some, like Miller, she suggests, defy imitation.

Decker's explanation is more sociopolitical. "Miller had rotten luck. As far as 'The Academy' is concerned, his moments were possibly the worst in terms of publicizing his work." When Miller's stuff was first being seriously considered in the United States, Decker continues, "American literary theory was under the hold of something called 'The New Criticism,' which is all about very tight, very regulated prose. That hurt him in the censorship trials; it was harder to find advocates for him because he wasn't using the style that was preferred at the time. Now, that's not true overseas. In France, in Japan, for instance, people talk of his work, but the Anglo-American critics do not." Then came the double whammy. "When Miller's type of prose did become popular, that's when Kate Millett and the Second Wave Feminists came in, and Miller was someone they only wanted to talk about in the pejorative sense. They overemphasized one facet of his work and ignored the rest. As a result, Miller lost the traction that had started to build because of earlier studies by William

A. Gordon and Ihab Hassan. He then became radioactive to nonfeminist mainstream criticism."

In a May 1969, letter to Kate Millett, reprinted in *Nexus* Volume 4 (2007), Miller wrote,

> Maybe it's simply a frightful lack of humor on your part which irritates me... If I could sum up what I mean in a few words it would be: I think you have missed the boat... Such writing may earn you another degree but I hardly think it will enhance the reader's understanding of my work.

Ouch.

MILLER AND THE ACADEMY

Decker speaks of what he calls "The Academy," or American academia, the way a zookeeper might refer to a wild and highly dangerous animal, with great respect for its insular nature and ability to protect itself. But Decker's focus looks beyond traditional narrow definitions.

"I don't care if you're in The Academy, if you are out of The Academy, if your interest is biography, if your interest is lesbian feminist readings of Miller. I don't care. We welcome you, and we will put you in our pages if it meets obvious editorial standards, and we will send them off to certain readers to make sure that they do."

Decker's guiding philosophy with *Nexus* is to avoid the heavy-handedness one might find elsewhere. "A lot of journals have very specific biases on how they want you to interpret or read an author's works. I felt that if we really wanted to stir the pot on Miller, particularly since not much had been done, we can't close our eyes to opinions that disagree with ours." This open approach to exploring Miller and his work leaves Decker's writers free to plumb Miller's seemingly fathomless literary depths.

For example, in *Nexus* Volume 7 (2010), Douglas Matus, in his essay "Teach as You Like and Die Happy: Henry Miller as High School Curriculum," suggests that

> Miller provides a bridge between the works of Whitman, Emerson, and Thoreau, and those of later writers like Jack Kerouac and Allen Ginsberg. American literature only fails to appear possessed of a clear lineage if the key figure of Miller is ignored.

Matus insists that

> teenage students find it difficult to connect to writing that feels personally remote. Miller's writing is so visceral, so persistently fresh and modern, that he serves as the ideal bridge between the literature of the 19th century and the concerns of today's youth.

As far as having any qualms regarding the exposure of young minds to Miller's more audacious material is concerned, Matus rejects the notion altogether. One need only "watch the reactions of a group of parents when their children are assigned 'objectionable' literature," to learn a valuable lesson about our contemporary intellectual society, he suggests.

> It does not matter that they allow their daughters to wear clothing that would make Miller's Parisian whores blush, or that their sons listen to music awash in obscenity. To see the word "fuck" or "cunt" on the printed page is enough to send them into hysterics.

His advice is to confront the accusation of obscenity head on. Bawdy humor, and the juxtaposition of the erotic and the holy, has a well-established place in literature, no matter how contemporary standards fluctuate. So be an adult, show an adult example, and get over it. But these incongruities in public perception should serve as a warning: These freedoms are vulnerable, at every level.

While it is rare to find a discussion of high school students' tastes in scholarly journals, it is even more rare to find scholars arguing with each other in a single volume. Decker, however, encourages it. He explains, "We don't care if you read one article, and then you read a second article and that second article contradicts the first one, because that's how an author's reputation gets cemented. Miller's not a one-trick pony, and he is complex and dynamic enough to support many competing interpretations."

Look at two articles that appear back to back in Volume 6 (2009). Richard Kostelanetz, in his piece "Henry Miller Decades Later," waltzes through some academic Freudian-Jungian interpretations of what makes an artist, then concludes that loving Miller's work is a young person's phase. "I learned from Miller much that I couldn't have learned anywhere else, initially about the writing of personal essays and perusing arts in addition to writing," he says, and recognizes how that early influence set him on a path of artistic and personal self-fulfillment. Although his point is well taken, I would encourage Kostelanetz to consider that those types of revelations might come to anyone at any age.

Following right behind Kostelanetz, however, is Maria Bloshteyn's "Writing the Underground," where, after a whirlwind eight-page synopsis of Dostoevsky's classic, *Notes from Underground*, she takes her time sussing out Miller's fictional narrator thusly:

It is not surprising then that the Henry Miller persona, living in an ultra-civilized society whose horrific twentieth-century present is the Underground Man's nightmarish future, should open "his" notes where *Notes from Underground* end... he is forced to take his underground where no one can see it—into his mind... Miller's underground man becomes a hero for our times, and the underground becomes one of the few places where personal survival and artistic creation is possible.

In other words, Bloshteyn claims that Miller created a boilerplate for the angst-riddled, alienated city dweller that would populate fiction for the next half century and beyond. Hardly the type of writing one would outgrow after high school.

Plowing the Field

"One of the things I'm proud about with *Nexus*," says Decker, "is that the writers have really plowed the field." In partnership with Miller collector Roger Jackson, each volume begins with a previously unpublished work by Miller himself. And there's plenty. Letters? Miller wrote thousands, as well as essays, and collaborative experiments with some of his contemporaries which never found their way into the many collections published during and after Miller's lifetime. The first-time publication of these makes each edition of *Nexus* an anticipated event for Miller scholars and his devoted readers hungry for something new.

The best of these so far, in my opinion, is "The New Instinctivism (A Duet in Creative Violence)." This piece, penned by Miller in collaboration with lifelong friend Alfred Perlès in 1931, was thought to be lost to posterity—so says Miller in his book *Letters to Emil*—but was discovered posthumously and printed in *Nexus*.

Edited and annotated by Karl Orend, "The New Instinctivism" is a surrealist-Dadaist-discordian farce, twenty-four pages long, and followed by Orend's notes, which take another fourteen pages, with nary an ibid. among them. These notes are an entertaining departure from the normally dry and uninteresting academic asides you find in most journals and biographies, and are representative of what you find after each and every piece throughout the *Nexus* series. Comprised of letters, histories, anecdotal information, and historical background, the notes supporting each piece are a worthy addendum to the series at large, and will be an invaluable resource for those writers, biographers, and Miller explorers who will inevitably follow.

Decker knows that, by now, the *Nexus* series has taken such a huge step forward in Miller criticism that any and all serious work on the author must inevitably come through the *Nexus* series to be viable. "Each author is responsible for his or her notes. I edit them when they come in," says Decker, "sometimes Roger, sometimes Karl. Karl loves his notes." In some cases, Decker and his collaborators will provide extra notes to an author's efforts lest any stone be left unturned.

As far as I can tell, the *Nexus* series breaks down into eight fundamental categories:

THE UNPUBLISHED MILLER

Mentioned above, these contain gems that make the series worth it to Miller fans all by themselves.

The Paris Miller of the 1930s

There are those, like Orend, who are dedicated to separating the factual Miller from the fictional one. These efforts are indispensable in realizing the creativity in his work and his giant contribution to his art. Only after we have defused the personal pronoun "I" in Miller's novels can we look at them as works of fiction apart from the man who wrote them. For some, The Paris Miller—the bold, quixotic, sexual adventurer and philosophic *flaneur* or wandering scholar—is the only Miller who matters.

Henry Miller, the Social Critic

Several writers in the *Nexus* series jump through hoops to prove Miller's anarchism. Although their arguments are compelling and extremely informative, I would argue that Miller's affection for anarchist writing was his way of seeking the kind of ideas that would enable him to liberate his own thinking, and therefore his own writing. Anarchy is a tricky concept. Even the *Encyclopedia of Philosophy* has a devil of a time giving a definition of it. Sympathy for an idea or philosophy does not an anarchist make. I would call him, instead, a *Discordian.* Perhaps a new word should be invented for Miller's unique form of disengagement politics—*Anacordian* perhaps?

Henry Miller, the Philosopher

In "Henry Miller and Jean Francois Lyotard: The Aesthetics of The Inhuman," Volume 5 (2008), Eric D. Lehman observes, "Scholars are just beginning to discover the usefulness of applying 'postmodern' philosophy to understanding Miller's work." Lehman uses a reading of the French philosopher Lyotard to make the point that "If postmodern thought questions, blurs, or even collapses the distinction between art and life, as it questions, blurs, or collapses so much of our traditional thinking, then, for better or worse, Miller is a postmodernist." Lehman then brings it home with two snippets from *Tropic of Cancer*:

> ...the task that the artist implicitly sets himself is to overthrow existing values, to make of the chaos about him an order which is his own... then it is that I run with joy to the great and imperfect ones, their confusion nourishes me... he who would create order, he who would sow strife and discord, because he is imbued with will, such a man must go again and again to the stake or the gibbet. I see behind the nobility of his gestures there lurks the spectre of the ridiculousness of it all—that he is not only sublime, but absurd.

Here then, is where the philosophies of Gilles Deleuze link hands with Nietzsche and Henry Miller, when Miller goes on to conclude,

> Once I thought that to be human was the highest aim a man could have, but I see now that it was meant to destroy me. Today I am proud to say that I am *inhuman*, that I belong not to men and governments, that I have nothing to do with creeds and principles. I have nothing to do with the creaking machine of humanity... Side by side with the human race there runs another race of beings, *the inhuman ones*, the race of artists who, goaded by unknown impulses, take the lifeless mass of humanity and by the fever and ferment with which they imbue it turn this soggy dough into bread and the bread into wine and the wine into song.

Because of Lehman's work, and others in the *Nexus* series, perhaps now, at last, Miller's Inhumans can take their rightful place between the Lost Generation and the Beats, where they belong.

HENRY MILLER, THE WRITER

Decker's book on Miller, *Henry Miller and Narrative Form*, explores Miller's unique usage of time, what Miller himself called Spiral Form. Says Decker,

> By filtering memories, dreams, and fantasies through an anecdotal matrix, Miller allows his narratives to blur categories of the past, present, and future, enabling him to depict a persona that stands both in and apart from the historical continuum. Such a framework lets Miller fuse real events and fabrications without sacrificing the "truthfulness" of his representations... Because his narratives deny strict chronology, Miller may rearrange the incidents of his life in a pattern that seeks not photographic realism, but psychological realism.

This accounts for the very subliminal feeling in most, if not all, of Miller's work, that what you are experiencing is in the here and now. This sense of immediacy is the deliberate use of Miller's own Spiral Form. I would like to think that someday entire academic creative writing curricula will be put forth to explore this exciting, and heretofore unexplored, genre. You can read more on this fascinating writing style, of course, in *Nexus* Volume 1 (2004), "Spiral Form and Henry Miller's Altered Ethics: Tropic of Capricorn Revisited," by Kenneth Womack, and D.A. Pratt's "On Reading Henry Miller's World of Sex," *Nexus* Volume 5 (2008).

THE MATURE MILLER

Here we meet the expatriate whose publishers, wanting a capitulating screed on the repatriation of the estranged artist, got instead *The Air-Conditioned Nightmare* and its sequel, *Remember to Remember*; the penetrating, almost whimsical Miller who wrote *The Wisdom of the Heart*; the older mature Miller, living in Big Sur high up on Partington Ridge, trying to shoo away beatniks and hippies while writing *Big Sur and the Oranges of Hieronymus Bosch*; the wizened veteran who took a look back at those early writings in the comprehensive retelling of *Capricorn* in *The Rosy Crucifixion* trilogy. This is a Miller I find myself returning to again and again. Here we find a man who has at last taken a deep breath, and is no longer attempting to get it all said with each sentence in each book.

THE REAL HENRY MILLER

"Miller was a master at caricature," observes Decker. "He actually wrote about that later in life. He said, 'I was writing about the scoundrel in myself.' And so yes, the blurring of the line between the 'scoundrel' and the more complete Henry Miller, is one that hasn't been challenged enough." In *Nexus*, writers like Orend, Lehman, J. Gerald Kennedy, Mark SaFranko, and others are doing just that. But it is clearly Karl Orend who is leading the charge. With at least one, often two or more pieces in several volumes, what emerges from Orend's investigations is a far different creature from the rogue, anarchistic discordian we meet in *The Tropics* and *The Rosy Crucifixion* and other works. Orend has instead discovered a three-dimensional figure, a man steeped in literature, multilingual, full of erudition, courage, and complexity.

The Real Henry Miller will charm and beguile you, and his tragic story will break your heart. Columnist Wambly Bald, part of the Miller circle in those early years in Paris (the Van Norden character in *Tropic of Cancer*), thought that Miller in person reminded him of Bert Lahr, who was famous for his role as The Cowardly Lion in *The Wizard of Oz*. Miller had seen Lahr on the vaudeville stage many times in New York. Bald remembered that, like Lahr, Miller was soft-spoken and never talked openly about his work. There was nothing about him, Bald says, to suggest he had great talent; he rarely stood out in a crowd, hiding behind a mask of easy affability and charm. Anaïs Nin in her diaries describes Henry in an apron, fastidiously keeping house.

For this reader, one of the most compelling aspects of the *Nexus* series is The Real Henry Miller. In all the years since he began his career, The Real Henry Miller is a man we are only now, thanks to Decker, being introduced to. This is the homeless intellectual, the man who abandoned everything to find his voice and use it come what may. In *Nexus*, the false impressions left over from his controversial past are exposed and one by one laid to rest. What remains is the full, rich life of a self-educated man who wrote what he pleased. It is a story of courage, suffering, and transcendence, "in every sense of the word."

The most chilling of all the articles depicting The Real Henry Miller is Orend's "The Observations Concerning His Morality and Probity Are Favorable: Henry Miller Glimpsed by the French Secret Service," *Nexus* Volume 4 (2007). Orend has unearthed a report by spies from the French secret service keeping an eye on intellectuals in pre-Nazi-occupied France, and how Miller's under-the-radar lifestyle may have saved his life.

Nexus's Self-Interrogations

Problems posed in earlier editions of *Nexus* are often resolved in later ones. In Volume 3 (2006,) Decker himself makes a cameo appearance in the journal, his only to date, investigating what happened to Miller's second wife, June, who is the subject of so many of his books. "There was a lot of speculation and interest in finding out what happened to June." When did she die? Where was she buried, and what happened to her after their marriage dissolved? So, Decker went to work, even hiring a private detective when he thought he was getting close. But the trail went cold. "So I went ahead and published my article and said 'if anyone knows anything let me know, and if there's no headstone, I'll pay for one.'" That's a sweet offer from a man living on a community college professor's salary. "Years went by, until someone posted anonymously on a Miller blog called *The Cosmodemonic Telegraph Company.*" June Mansfield/Miller died June E. Corbett, February 1, 1979, at the age of seventy-seven, and is buried in Valley View Cemetery in Cottonwood, Arizona. The story is published in *Nexus* Volume 7 (2010).

Richard Galen Osborne, or the Filmore character from *Cancer*, is another case in point. In *Nexus* Volume 5 (2008), Orend mentions that "Richard Galen Osborn died unknown and forgotten. No Miller scholar has even ever seen a photograph of him or knows where he is buried or when he died." Osborne's story is told, at last, in Volume 8 (2011).

While Decker and I are on the subject of scholarship's capacity to build upon its own investigations, he hands me a copy of Volume 8 and points to the photo on the cover. Henry is sitting at a dinner table with friends. A very young woman has joined him, clearly for the purpose of having her picture taken with the famous writer. "Who is she?" Decker wants to know, certain that sooner or later, an old photograph will turn up in someone's attic, or a name will drop from someone's memory, and yet another Miller mystery will be solved, and another puzzle piece will take its place in the ongoing reconstruction of this fascinating man's life.

On a personal level, I have been an ardent reader of Henry Miller for more than thirty years. Before the publication of *Nexus: The International Henry Miller Journal*, the only people with whom I could discuss his work were those to whom I had given his books. Now, we previously isolated and devoted readers have a community of our own at last (nexusmiller.org).

Joan Baez once said of Bob Dylan, "There's some people who'd say, you know, not interested. But if you are interested, he goes way, way deep." In that way, for people to whom Miller goes "way, way deep," the inclination is to regard him as a friend, more than a name beneath the title of a book. He becomes the wild and wise old uncle you never had, someone to help guide you through life's traumatic changes, someone who gives you permission to be yourself. Perhaps it's this quality that makes his readers simply want to call him *Henry*.

HERMES AT THE KAKISTOCRACY HOTEL

It is a late Sunday afternoon in downtown Atlanta. The Conference on Myth, Fantasy, and Imagination, on the last of its four days, is taking a breather between the afternoon lectures and mealtime festivities. The conference is a serious affair and most people are here because of their work. Psychologists, art therapists, writers, scholars, health care specialists, and people for whom lifting the lid of the psyche is a quest, a devotion, and for more than a few, a last resort. The book hall is largely textbooks. This is no Comicon. There is no pretending here to make-believe.

Tonight, after supper, the heavy hitters will take the stage. Poet Robert Bly, still going strong, along with Rumi translator and poet Coleman Barks, will square off tossing shards of verse at a very discerning audience who have learned the basics and are seeking something more. The two poets are, likewise, grizzled veterans who have been digging in these mines for a long time and bring to their presentation the freshness and ease that can only come from having touched every stepping stone along the way. Joined onstage by musicians playing cello, violin, and some type of zither, improvising along with their spoken verses to provide ambiance, the two masters are able to achieve the nearly impossible—to lift the audience out of time for a spell and show them a sacred hiding place, an open window, perhaps even a hint that a path might be found to some kind of salvation, or enlightenment, or peace.

Coleman Barks I knew only from his Rumi translations, but I wasn't a stranger to Bly's work, or his live reading persona. I greatly admired his book *Iron John*—a mythical travelogue through the primitive male psyche—and like-minded friends had given me audio books of the poet reading his work, which I listened to and savored on frequent cross-country drives.

Bly's reading style is almost theatrical, enhanced by his strange other-worldly voice that is rather nasal and high pitched for a big fellow—a Minnesotan thing perhaps. It suits him. It softens the gravitas he brings to his delivery. He will repeat a line or couplet over again when he wants the idea behind a phrase to sink in. He does this a lot. It's like the singing of a chorus. This repetition also has a soothing hint of mesmerism to it. You don't know when your feet have left the ground. That is the effect of working in parables, legends, myths, and allegories. He'll give you a dramatic reading of a poem, then, like a good teacher, read it again with repetitions, walking you through meanings, guiding you in deep. You thought you had a clue. You didn't. Now you do.

A favorite poet of Bly's is the Spaniard Antonio Machado, whom Bly has been translating. He recites Machado in his entrancing style first.

> The wind, one brilliant day, called
> To my soul with an odor of jasmine.
>
> "In return for my odor of jasmine,
> I'd like all the odor of your roses."
>
> "I have no roses; all the flowers
> in my garden are dead."

"Well then, I'll take the withered petals
and the yellow leaves and the waters of the fountain."

The wind left. And I wept. And I said to myself:
"What have you done with the garden that was entrusted
to you?"

And Bly looks up at the audience, his full, thick white hair, long and deeply parted at the side, and reads each stanza again:

The wind, one brilliant day, called
To my soul...
The wind, one brilliant day, called
To my soul with the odor of jasmine

"In return for my odor of jasmine,
I'd like all the odor of your roses.
In return for the odor of my jasmine,
I'd like all the odor of your Roses."

People who think easily in metaphor can teleport to the heart of poems such as this. But sometimes this repetition technique can help us access unfamiliar material or discover something beneath the obvious meaning of words. The audience and he are in that place now where personal truths float and swirl about the notion of the self. No secrets, no lies, no pretensions. Just being and time.

Coleman Barks and Bly then take turns reading and expounding, anecdotally blending their narratives, until the whole presentation is of a piece. Bly's work fits seamlessly in with Bark's Rumi translations and Rumi-inspired, more contemporary material. The well to which they return again and again is fathomless, the black water, deep down, unstirred for millennia.

The attendees at the Conference on Myth, Fantasy, and Imagination are serious people. By participating here, they hope to get a little of themselves back from the banal life-lessness of our downsliding culture. And that ultimately is a spiritual desire. If I have anything in common with these folks, it's a need to reacquire a sense of wonder, but with a mature longing for some kind of certainty. These notions aren't necessarily contradictory, at least not in the reprioritized world most attendees here would like to see come into being. The old hippie in me wanted to join right in. The writer in me, consequently, came away with a renewed sense of the marvelous, while at the same time longing for an assurance of sorts that my quest, or search for self, can proceed unmolested, and take me where it will.

By the afternoon before Bly and Barks do their thing, however, my brain is in dire need of a reset. I need a change of venue if only for a few hours. Almost everyone at the conference is eager to share whatever revelatory impressions of their own they are sorting through, but I now need other voices, or no voices at all.

The hotel itself is part of the problem. As magnificently huge as these corporate convention hotels can be, they often give me the creeps. Before long, the stark utilitarianism of these places starts to deaden the mind, and when the mind goes numb, the soul withers. Is architecture dead? Overhead are thousands upon thousands of square feet of empty space. But it's not empty. The same stale air is everywhere, as you can no longer open a window in a big hotel. I come to feel like I'm living on recycled carpet mites carried into my lungs by vacuum cleaner gas.

Strolling through the vaulted lobby, I realize that tomorrow this place won't be filled with quirky artists, peace-keepers, medicine women, and adventurers of mind and spirit, with their crazy hair and odd-looking clothes, carpet-bags and fanny pouches. More likely, the hotel will be full of insurance salesmen, money managers, construction firms, arms merchants. I've stood at a thousand modern metal bars like the one in the lobby here, struggling to find something interesting in whatever the flush-faced, bug-eyed business-person next to me has to say, and I shudder with prickly pique.

If a kakistocracy is rule of a society by the worst men in it, then this is their hotel. The Kakistocracy Hotel.

Clearly, I need to get out of here. So, I decide to venture out on foot. I go back to the room and put on a sport coat, pull a tie I wore the night before over my head, leave my collar loose, and make for the exit. As I cross through the lobby toward the main entrance, a gust of fresh air from the revolving front doors pulls me from the place, past the valet parking attendants, greeters, doormen, and bellhops, all lurking about with nothing to do. The street is deserted.

Sunday.

Downtown.

Business district.

Right.

I have always been attracted to the esoteric, to the poetry and philosophy of mysticism, and to myth. This is why I'm here. Study is one way to open the doors of this arena, and though largely self-taught, I like to seek out living poets and scholars who know their turf better than I do. Sometimes those doors are shut to outside inquirers, but once in a while they open for us without any effort at all. Throughout my life, I've been lucky enough to glimpse what I will call an inkling of The Divine through chance encounters with strangers. One cannot, however, orchestrate or premeditate or conjure such encounters; a neat bit of synchronicity is required. The best one can do is expect the unexpected. So, naturally, when you least expect it, here it comes.

Standing on the sidewalk, breathing in the fumes of an early twenty-first-century urban afternoon, I look right and left in search of a direction. Down the street, I spot the balcony of a restaurant, one story up, with an Old South filigree adorning the railings, homey and elegant, with lush thick vines hanging down. As I turn to make in that direction, a very large Black man steps deliberately in my path.

"I've got some bad news for you, little brother," he says as he falls in with me and we walk together.

"Well break it to me gently, will ya? I'm a little short on coping skills today," I smile, and by way of reassurance, I reach my hand up and grip his massive shoulder and give him a pat on the back.

He stops, I stop. He looks me deeply in the eyes.

"Ronald Reagan is dead."

It might not have been the last thing I would have expected him to say, but it sure as hell wasn't the first. He said it so gently, as though he thought I might fall to my knees in lamentation. I had to restrain myself from saying, "Good riddance, now let's get drunk!" I pause momentarily instead and take this guy in. He has stepped out of the world of strangers to give me the news. Why me, a middle-aged white guy in a jacket and tie, stepping out of a businesspersons' hotel? Did he think this was going to be bad news to me? He had no agenda that I could discern; there wasn't a hint of hostility in his face or tone, and as has happened to me many times before, it was as if the wily Greek messenger god Hermes was speaking to me through this man. Come to think of it, my stranger on the boulevard and I might actually have been close in age. Nineteen-sixties people of all stripes called each other brother and sister back in the day. This man and I might have more shared ideas than a superficial glance at the two of us might detect. "Little brother." I liked that. He made it sound familiar. I thought maybe it was.

I put my hand on his shoulder once more and say, "Well sir, I wouldn't wish Alzheimer's disease on anybody, and I've known some dear ones afflicted with it, and it's a big bad deal. But, to be honest, and forgive me if this sounds a little harsh, but in his case, I'm willing to make an exception. Welfare queens? Contras murdering socialists? Sympathy for abortion clinic bombers? Giant tax breaks for rich guys paid for by schoolkids, teachers, the mentally ill, wounded soldiers? I gotta tell ya big brother, I ain't gonna miss 'm."

We continue on for a bit in silence, our hands on each other's shoulders, like brothers, actually, the silence revealing a thousand cuts each.

"They said he didn't remember being president," the man said as we continued on down the street. We stopped and looked at the sky.

"Imagine that."

"Imagine that."

My father loved Reagan for cutting his taxes and could have cared less about the details. There were a lot of folks like my father. Reagan was their revenge on liberals whom they called "do-gooders," like doing good was a loathsome betrayal of their greedy creed. They sincerely believed these do-gooders had robbed them of their discretionary income only to give it away to losers and ne'er-do-wells who quite simply didn't deserve it. But my parents' generation had a lot more in common with the late president than mere fiscal hoarding might suggest, or some sophomoric rationale against accepting the responsibilities that come with wealth and what it means to our culture and community well-being at large.

I remembered sitting at another Kakistocracy Hotel in Washington, D.C., shortly after Reagan's reelection in 1984. At the table behind me a middle-aged Black man was interviewing a recent college graduate, a young Black woman, for a job in the administration. I overheard her come right out and ask him about the religious right, the saber-rattling, the welfare queens, and I can still hear him answer, "It is what it is. But if you want a job here, then you'll have to set all that aside." I still shudder.

The Reagan generation was born into a world where electricity, urban plumbing, and automobiles were new or not yet extant. There wasn't any radio, let alone television. My parents, both from small towns, truly believed that the world was so big you couldn't pollute it. Reagan himself believed that smoke went up the chimney and then simply disappeared. The Greatest Generation? That generation tried to destroy the world over and over again, with genocide, then with atomic weapons, then with chemicals. They stopped short from killing us all, or merely were forced to hit the brakes momentarily, thereby prolonging the agony of self-destruction, and we call them great for it.

My Hermes on the street corner then wondered, "If someone could have sat by Reagan's bed and told him what he had done, what might he have thought?"

Hmm.

We stood there, near the door to the restaurant with the appealing Southern balcony, for several more minutes until we had concluded our conversation. We shook hands, with a familial shoulder bump and hand clasp, and wished each other well. I could tell we were both wondering if we could, or even should, carry on. But that wasn't the thing to do. He crossed the street. I went inside.

The wind left. And I wept.
The wind left. And I wept. And I said to myself:
"What have you done with the garden that was entrusted to you?"

Myth, Fantasy, and Imagination, indeed.
The steak was delicious.

I'M THE GUY WHO (ALMOST) KILLED THE GUY WHO (ALMOST) KILLED ALBERT EINSTEIN

The Great Peace March for Global Nuclear Disarmament arrived in Washington, D.C., on November 15th, 1986. The participants had marched all the way from California to my hometown, the Capital of the Empire, to protest nuclear weapons. Under President Reagan, the war industry had shrugged off the negative image it had acquired during the Vietnam War. Now, saber-rattling politicians were postulating that nuclear war was something everyday citizens could speak of as a wise foreign policy option. After all, if you want to make astronomical amounts of money, the thing to do is to think astronomically. And the supersonic multi-nuclear warheaded MX missile, coming in at seventy million dollars a pop from the Raytheon Corporation, had the arms industry and all its dependents smiling, with stars in their eyes.

My two-man band, The Pheromones, had a steady group of regular venues where we played in and around D.C., as well as hot spots around the country. With songs like "The Great Rondini" (about our Teflon president), "Peace Once More," and "MX Madness," among others, we were the go-to guys if you wanted it topical, raw to the bone, and loaded with attitude. In other words, major media outlets wouldn't touch us, but fans came in all shapes and sizes. Members of the march's organizing committee had heard some of our anti-war numbers on the Pacifica radio station out in Berkeley. So, when the ragtag army of anti-war, anti-nuclear demonstrators were at last about to arrive at the nation's capital after walking three thousand miles, those friendly organizers put us at the top of the show, slipping us in at the last minute. We would play at the Lincoln Memorial, where later Sweet Honey in the Rock, Holly Near, and Ralph Nader would praise those marchers for their massive contribution to the cause.

While the marchers were gathering in Martin Luther King Park, we had enough time for a quick sound check. My stage partner Alvis Pheromone picked two songs I had written years earlier on Clovelly Island in Canada, "Grace in the World" and "Holiday," when even my closest friends didn't know I could write, play, or sing. I would sit on the porch overlooking the Lovesick Lake and play to the gently rippling tides. Now those two songs boomed out across the Reflecting Pool and bounced off the monuments, delivering an eerie kind of wonder and surprise at life's more ironic and unexpected twists and turns. We were standing where King had delivered his "I Have a Dream" speech. This memory still brings me happy chills.

Casey Kasem, a famous hit radio DJ, was the MC, and he called us up to the stage as the massive crowd of marchers was making its way to us from Martin Luther King Park and

Lafayette Square. There were already a thousand or more people gathered there—tourists, locals, and a bunch of fans who had found out we were playing I know not how, because, being last-minute additions, we were not on any schedule. But we could see the throng of marchers, a people's army, with their homemade banners, flags, and slogans, moving inexorably toward us with the slow determination of history itself. Our fingers were numb in the thirty-eight-degree cold, but we greeted them with songs: "Hey, Look Around You," "MX Madness," "The Great Rondini," "Money Go Round," "Host Homes," "Peace Once More," and "Galactic Funny Farm." Kasem brought us back for "Grace in the World."

As we stepped back from the mikes and took our bow, Kasem returned to talk to the crowd; we hurried over to put our guitars away as Sweet Honey in the Rock, an all-woman African American a cappela ensemble who just exude a kind of ancient life force, sang a spiritual welcome to our giant peace brigade, who were by now moving in that slow-surging not-to-be-denied way a large crowd moves, right up to the stairs of the Memorial.

As this was going on, at the back of the stage area, standing by our guitar cases, was Ralph Nader, flanked by two young acolytes, waiting for Kasem to introduce him. Now, this was long before Nader had torpedoed his liberal bona fides by running against Al Gore in the 2000 presidential election, still fourteen years distant, ensuring that stupid George W. Bush would become our president. But at the time, Nader was a genuine hero. I thought he could be another Abe Lincoln.

I approached Nader cautiously with an "is it okay?" look to his two handlers, who just smiled. I shook his hand and went on to explain that ten or more years earlier, I had bought a Chevrolet Monza that was a total lemon right from the first day I owned it. For example, the passenger door fell off—that's right, it just fell off. It happened on a first date with a lovely woman I had taken to the Kennedy Center for a concert. It was pouring rain, and when I got out to open the door for her, it simply tore off from its welded hinges and landed in the gutter. Do you know how fucking heavy a car door is? What's worse, my date insisted I take her home. So, with the car door sticking out of my hatchback, I drove her home with water pouring in her side. You'll be shocked to learn that our first date was our last. Also, that first year, a strut bar beneath the car fell off, and the entire chassis dropped down, grinding all four tires to pulp with only a few rotations. But I digress.

So, with a couple thousand people waiting, I stood there and told Ralph Nader about a time I was coming up the hill on Florida Avenue, in front of the Washington Hilton, when my brakes failed completely. I was yanking desperately on the emergency brake and pumping the brake pedal wildly and was able to bring the car to a stop but not until I had entered the crosswalk and bumped a man who angrily banged his fist on the hood of my car.

That angry man was Ralph Nader.

"It should have been a Corvair!" Nader laughed heartily, referencing his legal suit against the car company that made him famous and led to massive safety reforms in the auto industry that to this day have saved countless lives. He went on to tell a story of his own. Back in his college days in Germany, he was driving an old beater car with bad brakes, and rolling down a hill toward an intersection where he bumped an old man in his pajamas in the crosswalk. That man was Albert Einstein.

"So, in another life," he put his hands on my shoulders and smiled down at me, "You're the guy who killed the guy who killed Albert Einstein!" We both laughed hard. I then handed him two cassettes of our tunes, bootlegged to sell from the stage, with maybe eighty original songs. "Are all these songs different?" he wanted to know as only a true consumer activist would, and he tucked them into his jacket pockets. Then he calmly stepped up to a microphone and said, "I presume that by now, after your courageous experience walking all the way across the country for peace, many of you will go on to become active critics of the footwear industry."

It was a scream.

Nobody laughed.

Poor Ralph. Once upon a time, he was très cool.

That night we MCed a dance party for the marchers at a Nader event. When I recounted our conversation at the Memorial earlier that day, one of his aides laughed wearily, "Did he tell you his Einstein story? He tells that story to everybody!"

Now, I guess, so do I.

ACKNOWLEDGMENTS

My warmest affections and deepest thanks go to my Angels, Phantoms, and Gurus: Rose Solari, Nita Congress, Randy Stanard, Alan S. Johnson (AKA Alvis Pheromone, who also chipped in on the liner notes for the North Star Band), Andrew Beverina, who introduced me to Lucretius, Steve Waxman, Murray Freeburn, and Bob Dawson "Jimmy! Get over here!" James M. Decker, publisher of *Nexus: The International Henry Miller Journal*, who let me interview him from out of nowhere for three days, and his co-founder, Roger Jackson, a font of information on all things Miller. Ken and Theresa Butcher for keeping me sane in the spring, summer, and fall of 2022 on campus, Lakefield, Ontario, where the bulk of this writing went down, and we all got COVID.

In memoriam for those who have departed but are nestled lovingly, named or unnamed, in these pages: Max Rishor, Ella May Rishor, Dorothy Rose Patterson, Jack F. Patterson, Featherstonehaugh, Mark Noga (who pulled me out of a burning van and saved my life, then carried me broken and bleeding up the street banging on doors until someone took us in), and Dr. Marv Chadab (my beloved hockey buddy and WWI re-enactor).

And special thanks to Jim Salvie, for a super idea he gave me for my book *Bermuda Shorts,* twenty years or more before I got to use it.

And lastly, a word for Andrew Beverina, who said, "I'll give you twenty dollars, cash money, if you use the word PENIS in your next book." Consider this an invoice.

Nathan Leslie won the 2019 Washington Writers' Publishing House prize for fiction for his collection of short stories, *Hurry Up and Relax*. He is also the series editor for *Best Small Fictions*. Nathan's previous books of fiction include *The Invisible Hand, A Fly in the Ointment, Three Men, Root and Shoot, Sibs,* and *The Tall Tale of Tommy Twice*. He is also the author of a collection of poems, *Night Sweat*.

Nathan is currently the founder and organizer of the Reston Reading Series in Reston, Virginia, and the publisher and editor of the new online journal *Maryland Literary Review*. Previously he was series editor for Best of the Web and fiction editor for *Pedestal Magazine*. His fiction has been published in hundreds of literary magazines such as *Shenandoah, North American Review, Boulevard, Hotel Amerika,* and *Cimarron Review*. Nathan's nonfiction has been published in the *Washington Post,* the *Kansas City Star,* and the *Orlando Sentinel*. Nathan lives in Northern Virginia.

Works Cited

Part I: The Memory of Tomorrow

"The I Behind the I"
 Mercier, Pascal. *Night Train to Lisbon*. New York: Grove Press, 2018.
 Pessoa, Fernando. *The Book of Disquiet*. Edited and translated by Richard Zenith. New York: Penguin Classics, 2003.

"Do Conservatives Dream of an Electric Jesus?"
 Foner, Eric. *Tom Paine and Revolutionary America*. New York: Oxford University Press, 1976.
 Robertson, Ritchie. *The Enlightenment: The Pursuit of Happiness: 1680–1790*. New York: HarperCollins, 2021.

"Digby at the Swan"
 Wordsworth, William. *Selected Poems*. Edited by John O. Hayden. New York: Penguin Classics, 1994.

"Throwing in the Tao"
 Miller, Henry. *Tropic of Cancer*. New York: Grove Press, 1961.
 The Durrell-Miller Letters: 1930-1980. Edited by Ian S. McNiven. New York: New Directions, 1988.

Part II: The World of Yesterday

"Hermes at the Spouter Inn"
 Bryant, John. *The Cambridge Companion to Melville*. New York: Cambridge University Press, 2006.
 Jung, C. G. *Memories, Dreams, Reflections*. Translated by Richard and Clara Winston. New York: Pantheon Books, 1963.
 Melville, Herman. *Moby Dick*. Illustrated by Rockwell Kent. New York: The Modern Library, 1992.
 Miller, Henry. *Tropic of Capricorn*. New York: Grove Press, 1961.

"While Writing Roughnecks and Reading Moby Dick":
 Lawrence, D. H. *Studies in Classic American Literature*. New York: Penguin Books, 1961.
 Melville, Herman. *Moby Dick*. Ibid.
 Philbrick, Nathaniel. *Why Read Moby Dick?* New York: Penguin Books, 2011

"The World of Yesterday"

Eyffinger, Arthur. *"The Stars of Eternal Truth and Right": Bertha von Suttner's Campaigning for Peace, Social Justice, and Womanhood.* The Netherlands: Wolf Legal Publishers, 2013.

Illies, Florian. *1913: The Year Before the Storm.* Brooklyn: Melville House, 2013.

MacMillan, Margaret. *The War That Ended Peace: How Europe Abandoned Peace for the First World War.* New York: Random House, 2014.

Zweig, Stefan. *The World of Yesterday.* Translated by Anthea Bell. Lincoln: University of Nebraska Press, 2013.

"Stirring the Pot on Henry Miller"

Decker, James M. *Henry Miller and Narrative Form.* New York: Routledge, 2005.

Decker, James. M., Ed. *Nexus: The International Henry Miller Journal,* various volumes. www.nexusmiller.org

Decker, James. M., unpublished interview with James J. Patterson, summer 2011.

Hutchison, E. R. *Tropic of Cancer on Trial: A Case History of Censorship.* New York: Grove Press, 1968.

Miller, Henry. *Tropic of Capricorn.* Ibid.

Miller, Henry. *Black Spring.* New York: Grove Press, 1963.

"Hermes at the Kakistocracy Hotel"

The Rag and Bone Shop of the Heart: Poems for Men. Edited by Robert Bly, James Hillman, and Michael Meade. New York: HarperCollins, 1992.

Thanks are due to the following publications in which the following essays originally appeared, sometimes in slightly different form:

Gargoyle Magazine: "Hermes in the Bathtub."

The Maryland Literary Review: "Hermes at the Spouter Inn" and "The Memory of Tomorrow."

Nexus: The International Journal of Henry Miller Studies: "Throwing in the Tao: Henry Miller as Life Coach, Literary Instructor, and Spiritual Guide."

Music Gigs Gone Wrong, an anthology from Paycock Press: "Who's a Good Boy?"

"The Band That Time Forgot" originally appeared as the liner notes for the double album *Then and Now* by the North Star Band.

Robert Bly's translation of Antonio Machado's poem, "The wind, one brilliant day, called," is reproduced with permission from the Robert Bly Estate and Ruth Bly.

The quote from Margaret MacMillan's *The War that Ended Peace* is reproduced with permission from the author and Penguin Random House.

Alan Squire Publishing is an independent literary press founded in 2010 to publish books of fiction, nonfiction, and poetry that are beautifully written and beautifully made, with the avid reader and book lover in mind. We are committed to bringing to the public books of great merit that deserve a wide readership, and to forging a new model of collaboration with other independent presses here and abroad.

In 2015, we founded our Legacy Series, devoted to career-spanning collections by writers who meet the following three criteria: the majority of their books have been published by independent presses; they are active in more than one literary genre; and they are consistent and influential champions of the work of other writers, whether through publishing, reviewing, teaching, mentoring, or some combination of these. Modeled after the "readers" popular in academia in the mid-twentieth century, our Legacy Series allows readers to trace the arc of a significant writer's work in a single, representative volume.

Our collaborators on various book projects include Left Coast Writers in San Francisco, California, Chris Andrews Publications, Ltd., in Oxford, England, and the Santa Fe Writers Project, now based in Bethesda, Maryland.

We also have an online literary magazine, theaspbulletin.com, founded in 2020, that publishes poetry, fiction, creative nonfiction, and the occasional interview.

All ASP titles are distributed internationally by Independent Publishers Group (IPG), the original independent book distributor in the United States. For bulk orders, visit them here: http://www.ipgbook.com/

And we love working with book clubs, independent bookstores, and all other venues and means of getting our books into the right hands. You can contact us directly about such things via our website, alansquirepublishing.com.

Our Titles So Far:

That Paris Year, by Joanna Biggar (novel), 2010

Bermuda Shorts, James J. Patterson (essays) 2010

A Secret Woman, by Rose Solari (novel), 2012

Billy Christmas, by Mark A. Pritchard (novel), 2012

Roughnecks, by James J. Patterson (novel), 2014

The Last Girl, by Rose Solari (poetry), 2014

Difficult Weather, by Rose Solari (poetry), expanded 2nd edition, introduction by Katherine E. Young, 2014

The Richard Peabody Reader, A Legacy Series Volume, introduction by Michael Dirda, 2015

Chaos Theories, by Elizabeth Hazen (poetry), 2016

Other Voices, Other Lives: A Grace Cavalieri Collection, A Legacy Series Volume, introduction by Rose Solari, 2017

Scattered Clouds: New and Selected Poems, by Reuben Jackson, introduction by Abdul Ali, 2019

Melanie's Song, by Joanna Biggar (novel) 2019

Navigating the Divide: Selected Poetry and Prose, by Linda Watanabe McFerrin, A Legacy Series Volume, introduction by Joanna Biggar, 2019

Girls Like Us, by Elizabeth Hazen (poems), 2020

Woman Drinking Absinthe, by Katherine E. Young (poems), 2020

Red Riviera: A Daria Vinci Investigation, by David Downie (novel), 2021

The Other Ones, by Dave Housley (novel), 2022

let the dead in, by Saida Agostini (poems), 2022

Roman Roulette: A Daria Vinci Investigation, by David Downie (novel), 2022

Junk Shop Window: Essays on Myth, Life, and Literature, by James J. Patterson, 2023

Already Gone: Forty Stories of Running Away, edited and with an introduction by Hannah Grieco, forthcoming, September 2023